MOSAIC THEATRE

MOSAIC

THEATRE

The Creative Use of
Theatrical Constructs

Lael J. Woodbury
Dean, College of Fine Arts
and Communications
Brigham Young University

Brigham Young
University Press
Provo, Utah

Library of Congress Cataloging in Publication Data
Woodbury, Lael Jay, 1927–
  Mosaic theatre.

  Bibliography: p. 193
  Includes index.
  1. Theatre — Production and direction. I. Title.
PN2053.W6   792·.023   76-31604
ISBN 0-8425-0542-3

Library of Congress Catalog Card Number: 76-31604
International Standard Book Number: 0-8425-0542-3 (cloth)
© 1976 Brigham Young University Press. All rights reserved
Brigham Young University Press, Provo, Utah 84602
Printed in the United States of America
76   2Mp   .5Mc   13410

To Margaret

Real art will be found only when it has been freed from the dictates of an art-form foreign to it.

V. I. PUDOVKIN

CONTENTS

ACKNOWLEDGMENTS

I gratefully acknowledge those who, in addition to the authors cited, have in one way or another affected the content of this book— Raymond, Wanda, Lavar, Delma Rae, Kippi, Shannon, Jordan, Lexon, Harold, Barney, Charles, and Lorin.

I'm grateful, too, to Helen Pomeroy and Louise Hanson who helped prepare the manuscript; to Neal Maxwell, Dallin H. Oaks, Robert K. Thomas, and Ben E. Lewis for their confidence and encouragement; and to the Karl G. Maeser Associates for the BYU Creative Arts Award which provided means for accelerating this study and testing its conclusions.

MOSAIC THEATRE: AN INTRODUCTION

The playwright is considered by many the peerless creator of today's theatre art. Once written, his language-work is interpreted by the director and expressed — that is, made concrete or objective — on the stage by physical elements such as actors, movement, color, light, and sound. His artwork usually presents human characters in a chronological story or action, although contemporary productions often rearrange time and space for aesthetic effect.

But his is not the only conceivable form of theatre art. How limited music would be if it were restricted to the eight tones of the Western octave! Today's music consists of the artful amalgamation of abstract sounds derived from any source. Today's graphic artist not only paints recognizable form, he also shapes into art the very constructs, the design elements, from which life forms are made. And contemporary ballet, which traditionally presented story in movement form, now consists of movement and space equivalents of the sounds (music), colors, and physical forms from which traditional ballet is made.

Mosaic Theatre explains why, with the responsive mechanism of the modern theatre available to him, the theatre artist, too, need not limit his artistry to traditional methods and substance. It challenges the premise that language is the essential construct of theatre, and that the playwright is the premier theatre artist. If that was once true, it need not be so now. Nor is story or Aristotelian action necessarily the best structural device.

It suggests an alternative concept and form of theatre art — one more appropriate to our level of technology and at least as rich as language-drama in sources for theatrical expression.

It describes, too, certain principles by which the theatre's media can be organized artfully, and it provides examples of how these principles have been, or can be, implemented in production. These examples, usually presented at the ends of chapters after general principles have been discussed, comprise a list or compilation of models or suggestions intended to inspire the reader and to show him that the application of the principle to

1

From Jarka Burion's *Scenography of Josef Svoboda*. Wesleyan University Press, 1971.

theatrical production is possible and potentially artful.

Mosaic Theatre is divided into three parts. THE CREATOR, chapters one and two, is a rationale for a new art of theatre; THE CONCEPTION, chapters three and four, is a description of the conceptualizing process — whether, as in traditional drama, based on the written script, or derived, in an inverse manner, from a close analysis and innovative structuring of the theatre's expressive media; THE EXPRESSION, chapters five through eleven, is an exploration of the artistic principles with which the director of *any* theatrical piece might express a concept. The book is addressed to the director who practices the inverse method of artistic conception described in chapter four, but it is equally useful to the director of language-drama.

I do not envision in the near future a widespread departure from traditional theatrical practice representing 2,500 years of experience. It is man-centered, and its conventions are familiar and workable. But there are theatre artists and patrons eager to expand the medium. They realize that current technology provides them with a newly expressive mechanism, and they intend to explore its potential for artistic expression, hoping as they do to discover ideas, insights, and experiences never before conceived, and to share them in innovative artistic works.

*In my view, no one has the right
to call himself author, that is to
say creator, except the person who controls
the direct handling of the stage.*

ANTONINE ARTAUD

THE CREATOR

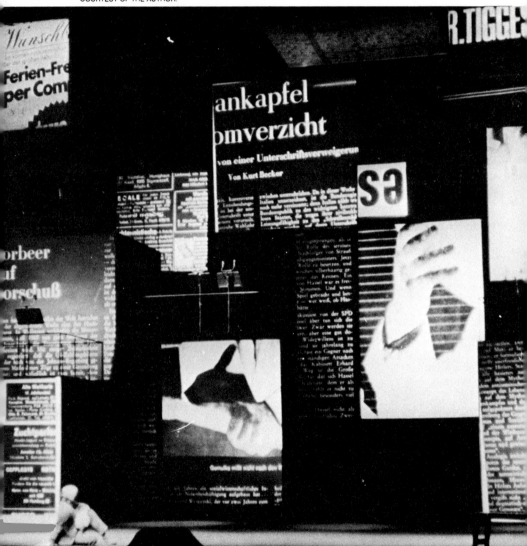

A profoundly visual production of *The Journey*. From Jarka Burion's *Scenography of Josef Svoboda*. Wesleyan University Press, 1971.

1
THE RESPONSIBILITY FOR FORM

Among theatre artists, the right to control form is supremely important. Actors, conjecturing that action antedates language, claim that their art generated the other parts of theatre. And they have shown ability to control form; written drama merely displayed the Greek actor's technique in the fourth century B.C., and classic Roman actors virtually discarded language in favor of action. Renaissance — and nineteenth-century — professional actors even decided their plays' specific content during the course of performance. The actor has managed artistic authority so well, in fact, that he has proved his ability to write without the other parts of theatre — requiring only performance space.

If, then, theatre art consists of artistic stimulation and perception, and if that stimulus — the revealed object — is always the living actor, he should fix form because the art of acting is the essence of theatre which other arts of theatre augment. But if we distinguish between the living actor and other things revealed, actors are dispensable. In Samuel Beckett's *Play,* the living actor assumes a machinelike condition from which he delivers the play's language in a toneless, mechanical manner. In the musically induced colors and forms in Walt Disney's *Fantasia,* in light and color modulated electronically by the quality and force of the human voice, and in the *Son et Lumière* productions, where no man-figure appears, are kinds of theatre in which actors have no place. Theatre must reveal, but it need not reveal actors or human forms.

Historically the playwright challenges the actor's artistic authority, claiming for himself the right to fix form. And there have been periods such as the mid-seventeenth century in France and Italy and during the popularity of nineteenth-century French melodrama when the essence of theatre dwelt neither in performed characters nor in the script but in visual artistry and effect.

Today a different premise prevails: designers and actors interpret, embellish, and express, but they no longer control the forms of the artistic statement. Actors and designers now agree that they are artistically interdependent. They view the playwright as the theatre's chief creator and see his play, the written script, as theatre's essence.

7

This point of view is widespread; it has been expounded for centuries by advocates for whom language is the chief medium of expression. Their rhetoric, especially because it can be collected and preserved, constitutes a sizeable and impressive body of opinion.

This trend again toward control of form by the playwright pleases many, for the playwright has been meanly used by theatre artists who live by his creativity. Economic and social forces and the collaborative and thus adulterated characteristics of the theatre complex have so compromised the playwright's artistic status that he became and still is, in the opinion of some: "the ultimate whore of the theatre."

Nevertheless, the playwright's position as arbiter of form was never so strong as now. If some few see the playwright as a collaborative artist only, equal in creativity to the actor or designer,[1] a more typical view is implied by Worthington Miner's advice to his fellow directors: "The one thing a director should not be is 'creative. . . .' A director is only a substitute for an author's executive weakness."[2]

Copyright laws certainly assume the artistic validity of playwright as form maker. Though they have not changed appreciably since 1909, they are now being revised even more to the writer's advantage. Already precedent-setting interpretations are rigidly favorable to the playwright's will, sufficiently so that under existing law no production of Eugene O'Neill's *Long Day's Journey Into Night* is authorized until the producer promises explicitly that each word in the script will be delivered. Furthermore, if the copyright statements which now preface scripts describe the law ("Owners of copyright, not producers, must decide when a classroom or studio performance or reading is actually private"[3]), playwrights themselves have judiciary authority to interpret the scope and application of copyrights.

---

1. "It is theatre which is the main art; and the acting, and the play, and a third thing [the stage] are all equally contributive." Richard Southern, *The Open Stage* (London: Faber and Faber, n.d.), p. 10.

2. Worthington Miner, "Directing the Play," in *Producing The Play,* ed. John Gassner (New York: The Dryden Press, 1941), pp. 211, 217.

3. Norris Houghton, ed., *Laurel Masterpieces of Continental Drama* (New York: Dell Publishing Co., 1963), 1:221.

Plays as literature, of course, are personal artworks, and copyrights protect their integrity. Literary art is the verbal equivalent of an artistic vision upon which the imposition of a second artist's vision and execution is unthinkable. The writer's absolute right to control the disposition of his work is beyond challenge.

The playwright, however, unlike many writers, creates more than literature, and because it is more, it is not precisely literature. Essentially the playwright is an extra-literary artist. He uses the stuff of literature to create form which demands embodiment in performance. This is a fundamental point many playwrights reject.

William Gibson's *The Seesaw Log,*[4] for example, illustrates his muddy distinction between the arts of theatre and literature. He began rehearsing *Two For The Seesaw* with the novelist's assumption that literature is the theatre's art. He challenged the convention that the performance is the measure to which directors, actors, and the script, too, must yield, and although production circumstances forced him to quiet his revolt, he did so under protest and with ill will between himself and his collaborators. Periodically he resolved to write only novels henceforth expressly to preserve the integrity of his vision. Apparently he still is unhappy about the theatre's unique demands, for he inserted in the published script segments which were deleted from the original production. It is this literary version, presumably, that he authorizes others to produce.

Mr. Gibson's experience affirms the fact that without performance a play is unrealized, a fact playwrights acknowledge when they seek production of their work, for production is redundant if language fully expresses the playwright's concept. It is possible, in a way, to study only the literary aspects of a play, but in that view one sees not the realization but the potential of vision. Thus the moment the playwright commits a script to performance, whenever he decides to express through the medium of theatre instead of language only, he animates potential adulteration as well as artistic life. It is his loss of absolute control of form — not required of most literary artists —

---

4. William Gibson, *The Seesaw Log* (New York: Alfred A. Knopf, 1959).

which playwrights deplore and copyright laws do not tolerate.

It is important, then, in the interests of theatre art, to determine if final control of production form rightfully belongs to the playwright. Whether the playwright may specify the exact use made of his product is not the question; he owns what he creates. The question is do current legal and philosophical trends to reinforce the playwright's form-determining power serve either his purpose or those of the theatre?

Whatever their rights, playwrights themselves are chary of the restrictions they impose upon others. They modify their scripts themselves when rehearsals indicate that what they wrote does not appear as intended. Their revisions may not be guided merely by a desire to create a commercially successful production; perhaps from observing and hearing their drama performed they discover a richer, more dramatic expression of theme. Significantly, playwrights repeat this process with each production of the same script on which they collaborate, no matter how refined as literature the script becomes, for production conditions and performance artists are never equal.

Even Eugene O'Neill, described by Arthur Gelb as an unusually dedicated novelist-playwright more interested in printing than in producing his plays, sanctioned script modifications when he saw that not doing so jeopardized the artistic quality of a production.[5] But his copyright restrictions do not extend that same freedom to today's producers of *Long Day's Journey Into Night*. They are an unreasonable burden upon artists who admire and wish to stage it. Even if this stipulation was specified by O'Neill himself, it imposes a restriction inconsistent with his own practice.

When the playwright is dead or unavailable, copyright and ethical problems press heavily upon directors, actors, and designers who respect the author's product and wish to do artful service with it. "The play is now a finished work," they are told. "Its Broadway form, now printed, is its final form, and it is copyrighted to protect it from unauthorized revision." While it is clear that the living

5. "Onstage He Played the Novelist," *New York Times Book Review*, 30 August 1964, p. 1.

playwright has a moral and legal right to change his own property (and that he will do so when rehearsing revivals of his plays), it is equally clear that performers deprived of his presence must work with neither his counsel nor his authority to modify the script.

Fortunately some playwrights — Arthur Miller and Maxwell Anderson among them — are sufficiently knowledgeable about theatre to encourage that creativity which their copyrights withhold. Arthur Miller wrote: "When I see a play whose dialogue is fine but cluttered with unnecessary words, I have the impulse to get up and crush out the impeding elements. My reaction is, it would have been better if the director hadn't been so damn subservient to the playwright."[6] This astonishing and refreshing advice, although carefully limited to directors of scripts "cluttered with unnecessary words," hardly represents the typical playwright's philosophy as manifest in copyright law, but it does reveal Miller's healthy recognition that theatre and the playwright are better served by a creative artist than a legal device.

The matter is critical when we revive a play of dated structure or theme. A single reel of a 1936 movie illustrates the changes in taste that have occurred since then, the year in which Maxwell Anderson's *Winterset* was introduced. One director, interested in staging *Winterset* but conscious of his legal and ethical responsibilities, wrote to Anderson before his death and asked for permission to shorten or revise several of Mio's and Miriamne's final speeches. Mr. Anderson telegraphed: "Go ahead — if you think you're a better playwright than Maxwell Anderson."

The director knew better, but he knew also what playwrights can never know for all productions: the audience and its tastes, the cast and its talent. He opened with the scene uncut — at which the audience laughed. But with Anderson's permission the director deleted lines and simplified action through successive performances until, after the fourth one, Mio and Miriamne exchanged only a few words before dying from brief bursts of gunfire, thus providing a

---

6. "Arthur Miller Ad-Libs on Eliz Kazan," *Show* (January 1964), p. 98.

terse, believable, and moving ending to the play and rendering service to its author. Possibly another, more competent cast could perform the final scene as printed and make it acceptable to today's tastes, but that possibility could not alter this director's circumstances. His limited group needed at least as much creative freedom as that accorded the larger talents of Broadway.

A moral problem appears when we choose a play in the public domain. With no copyright inhibitions, the dilemma of our artistic and ethical relationship to the script stands in high relief. If a printed script is a completed work whose form is forever fixed, then whoever modifies the least segment of any play, classic or otherwise, lacks artistic integrity.

On the other hand, our responsibility to the audience is funda-mental. As described by Hugh Hunt: "He [the director] must so adjust his production that the difference of outlook between one age and the other does not mar or weaken the enjoyment of the play, and at the same time he must give due emphasis to the ritualistic qualities which the plays have come to assume in the minds of the audience."[7]

Even if one sees himself exclusively as an interpretive artist whose responsibility is to act as the absent playwright's executive, he does the best by making the script's production meaningful to the audience. But what meaning is he to convey? Presumably the script's meaning. But a classic script may not be altered ethically even to clarify meaning unless we can do the same to a copyright play with moral impunity.

A capable actor might perform the main body of a role well despite technical demands —a laugh, a scream, a dance, invective— which he renders poorly. But presumably he is the best artist available for the role. Shall the director cancel the production because an actor's technique is flawed? Is an actor's technique ever adequate to render a role perfectly? Curtis Canfield explains:

---

7. *The Director in the Theatre* (London: Routledge and Kegan Paul, 1954), p. 110.

*The fact remains that . . . the acting talent necessary to sustain
audience interest unflaggingly for more than two and a half hours
[is a scarce commodity], particularly in the amateur theatre and the
professional theatre below the first rank. There is much to be said
for the director who insists on taking the precaution to hold down the
acting time to two hours. How many of us have had to suffer through
long-drawn-out productions where judicious (and extensive) cutting
would have been an act of mercy not only for the audience but for the
cast as well.*[8]

That such honest counsel to alter playscripts can appear in this
and other reputable books on directing is evidence of the disparate
views held by directors and playwrights. This viscid dilemma urges
the need for appraising the trend toward rigid copyright laws and for
an assignment of executive authority that we can practice as well as
prescribe. It is one thing to teach, preach, and legislate inviolable
copyrights; it is another to produce plays under conditions that pose
a moral dichotomy.

Assignment of form to the playscript, manifest in theory and
copyrights, is self-defeating. The playscript does not control
production form. The script controls only the form of language,
language which is a means to the end of performance. It is merely a
part of the whole.

But if not the script, who shall determine the form of theatre art,
the exact performance which is the art work? He who conceives it
will know its form. Gordon Craig and others have urged the
playwright to go beyond writing the script and supervise the theatre's
expression of his concept in the concrete language of the stage,
thus assuring his right and responsibility to fix form. Few playwrights
have attempted so much, perhaps because their talent is linguistic,
incapable of manipulating the tangible elements of the theatre
complex and the intangible creativity of the actor. But unques-

---

8. *The Craft of Play Directing* (New York: Holt, Rinehart and Winston, 1963), p. 246.

tionably it is the way to assure purity of form from concept to expression.

If, however, the script cannot and the playwright will not determine performance form, where shall we assign responsibility? The answer to that question cannot be structured upon traditional premises, for they were established to animate a concept of theatre severely lacking today's means for exact expression. Without today's means, without command of the several stimuli — such as electric light — which the spectator apprehends, artists of the past could only manipulate those communicative stimuli (sound and movement) that they did control. But today's theatre is such an expressive mechanism that now precise control of virtually all significant stimuli is possible.

Having this machine, an unprecedented medium in which vision, hearing, odor, temperature, and proximity are variable, we are not unlike Lev Kuleshov, Russian painter and film theorist. In 1922 when analyzing the expressive potential of projected-photography machines, he realized that he must discover the essential substance of cinematography before he could compose that substance artfully. Substance determines product, he reasoned. Five hundred years before Christ, this same logic had brought Chinese philosopher Lao-Tze to conclude that the substance of architecture is not walls and roofs but space. In our time, Frank Lloyd Wright revolutionized the art by reiterating the philosophy of "organic" architecture, the conviction that form follows function.

Kuleshov questioned the prevailing belief that the function of the camera is to see for an absent spectator. If this is true, any artistry of filmmaking occurs in front of the camera; the camera itself merely records action as an immobile viewer would see it from an ideal position. But then we have photographed theatre art, not necessarily cinematic art. As a new medium, film can express what before its invention had been technically unfeasible. If language can express poetry through the juxtaposition of verbal images, cinema can express poetry through juxtaposed visual and aural images. Therefore, reasoned Kuleshov, the *fundamental construct* of cinematic art is not language-drama but film, and the crucial art of filmmaking takes place not in front of the camera but in the cutting room where film, not actors or language, is composed to express the artistic vision.

Today's theatre is not unlike Kuleshov's new medium. To the extent that we can exercise meticulous control of what the audience hears — including elaborate amplified or subliminal sound images and qualities, to the extent that we can direct or even force the audience to see specifically those visual images we design, our theatre is a versatile as cinema. In the sense that we can vary the actor's or the stage's proximity to the audience, adapt the performance to the occasion, and appeal to the audience's sense of touch (through resonances and vibrations possibly) and smell if we wish, our machine is superior to cinema as now used.

What, then, is theatre's fundamental construct? We can create without the living actor. Nor are settings, lights, or costumes mandatory for an artistic theatrical statement. Perhaps our machine, the theatre complex, is now so advanced as to emancipate us from the dependence upon language which characterized the Greek and Elizabethan theatre.

Playwrights, critics, and scholars will reject this assumption, for they are linguistically oriented. It is the writer's genius that he chooses language before other communicative media such as color, gesture, and abstract sound to express his vision or experience. That is his genius, and his limitation. For theatre depicts experience, not its language equivalent. It presents an action, not its description — in present, not past tense. Language, the stuff of scripts, is not experience. It is a summary, a description, a symbol or an evocator of experience. We experience movement, sound, and color, but (except for their musical qualities) we interpret words.

Not all theatrical events are alike, of course. For some purposes language is the only thinkable medium, and I neither restrict nor deprecate its use. But I do suggest greatly expanded use of the communicative means of the modern theatre which go beyond language. "Don't tell me that the mother falls down the stairs; show it to me," epitomizes the film artist's attitude toward language.

We can learn much from cinema's history and techniques. David Wark Griffith explicated thought by bringing a camera close to a player's eyes, then depicting on the screen the object of his thoughts. By showing the trembling hands of the actor he conveyed emotional states. V. I. Pudovkin demonstrated that juxtaposed images, such as shots of a prisoner intercut with shots of a sunlit brook, birds, and a laughing child, can, like a word-poem, develop new images, feelings, or meanings within the viewer representative of the prisoner's anticipation of freedom. Abstract sound can parallel or even recreate the processes of thought (see chapter ten).

How like this cinematic philosophy is our habit of "seeing" a play. We purchase admission to hear a concert, but we go to see, not to hear, a play. And when we leave, we remember what happened — the incidents, not especially what was said; for "in theatre, everything must transform into the visible and sensible."[9] How remarkable that in today's theatre we fix permanently the diction (an element of drama that Aristotle placed fourth) and leave the form of the action — the incidents — (which Aristotle placed first) to the discretion of *interpretive* artists.

Antonine Artaud saw the problem more clearly than most writers:

In the theatre as we conceive it, the text is everything. It is under-stood and definitely admitted, and has passed into our habits and thinking; it is an established spiritual value that the language of words is the major language. But it must be admitted even from the Occidental point of view that speech becomes ossified and that words, all words, are frozen and cramped in their meaning, in a restricted schematic terminology. For in the theatre as it is practiced here, a written word has as much value as the same word spoken. To certain theatrical amateurs this means that a play read affords just as definite and as great a satisfaction as the same play performed. Everything concerning the particular enunciation of a

---

9. Friedrich Duerrenmatt, quoted by Randolph Goodman, *Drama on Stage* (New York: Rinehart and Winston, 1961), p. 381.

*word and the vibration it can set up in space escapes them, and
consequently, everything that is capable of adding to the thought.
A word thus understood has little more than discursive, i.e.,
elucidative, value. And it is not an exaggeration to say that in view
of its very definite and limited terminology the word is used only to
sidestep thought; it encircles it, but terminates it; it is only a
conclusion.*[10]

I have labored the point because it is fundamental. Playwright
Edward Albee will disagree with me, probably, for he has said: "The
play exists in its total and real form on the typewritten page, where it's
three-dimensional. When you start working with it on a stage with
actors, it becomes artificial, and then it's gradually brought back to
reality."[11] His attitude perpetuates the fallacy that there is something
untouchable about language as one of theatre's media.

But against this assessment of language as the substance of
theatre art, Max Reinhardt speaks of the "tyranny" of literature over
the stage. Perhaps, after all, an author should not be concerned
about how a director succeeds, so long as he does succeed with the
author's intent.

------

10. Mary Caroline Richards, trans., *The Theatre and Its Double* (New York:
Grove Press, 1958), pp. 117–18.
11. "The Talk of the Town," *The New Yorker* (19 December 1964), p. 33.

Orchestrated visual stimuli.

2
THE CONTROL OF FORM

The problem of language's significance in the theatre is consequential. If the verbal script is the indispensable element of the medium, then the theatre is essentially a language art.

Surprisingly, while most observers think of actions and actors as central to theatre, many have come to different conclusions. Hugh Hunt argues that *the story* is fundamental. (If this concept is accurate, theatre artists must subordinate all means to the expression of story, even if, conceivably, some language — as in cinema — must be deleted.) On the other hand, Granville-Barker defines *acting* as the fundamental construct; Erwin Piscator ascribed that characteristic to *theatre's social purpose,* and Max Reinhardt prized *the director's ideas* engendered by the script as fundamental. Indeed, Alan Schneider told me that he sees *the beat* as the stuff from which theatre is made.

No doubt each man is right within his context. But the implications of any of these emphases are profound. The present general acceptance of the written script as essence accounts in large measure for the playwright-director rivalry for artistic control.

Looking beyond these constituents of theatre — setting, language, actors, story — we must see the theatre fundamentally as a complex machine for controlling perception, kin in that respect to the arts of painting and music; and the purpose of any creative artist is to manipulate those stimuli which reach the perceptor in such a way as to engender within him a reasonably predetermined response. This, of course, is one reason for framing a picture, to define pertinent stimuli. A musician calculates the acoustical properties of his recital hall for the same reason — to control stimuli. The visual arrangement of printed poetry can be an additional attempt to monitor perception. The theatre, a complex apparatus for conveying stimuli, is a unique, monolithic medium of expression which transcends language, movement, or any of the individual stimuli with which it expresses artistic vision.

Again, that vision is not spoken language. Speech is itself a stimulus requiring organization. The vision is the view, the insight, the unique apprehension of the creator-organizer, by whatever name, and it is that vision which informs all choice of expressive stimuli, including language, during the preparation of the theatre art-object. *Thus expressive sensory stimuli are the substance of art, whose form is determined by whoever organizes and controls them.* The theatre complex is the means by which the theatre artist stimulates, and the performance is the medium of stimulation — the art work.

Suppose that the playwright conceives the vision and expresses it only in language — that he declines personally to translate that vision into the necessarily concrete media of the stage. Whoever supervises the theatrical expression can never know the playwright's vision perfectly. The fact is so patent that Jacques Copeau's famous statement concerning the director — "He does not invent ideas, he recovers them" — is absurd. If recovery is possible, why do no two interpretations of a script mirror each other? To be recoverable, ideas, even forms, must be immutable. The problem is so real that Margaret Webster said of the world's most studied plays (the ideas of which would be universally recovered by now if to do so were possible):

I have written and repeated many times in public that I feel very deeply and increasingly as my theatrical experience widens and deepens, that no one is qualified to make the final pronouncement on Shakespeare: neither in the classroom nor in the theatre has anyone the right to say: "this is the right way — the only way — of interpreting Shakespeare, this is the right way of producing such and such a play, such and such a scene, such and such a part."[1]

Even if the idea were once performed to Shakespeare's satisfaction (which does not necessarily mean that the original idea was perfectly recovered), subsequent productions inevitably express values not present in the first. Again Miss Webster: "It would be foolish for Helen Hayes to have tried to play the part (of Olivia) with

---

1. "Shakespeare and the Modern Theatre" (Fifth lecture of the Helen Kenyon lectureship at Vassar College. Delivered June 1, 1944), p. 5.

the kind of romantic glamour with which I imagine (for I never saw them) Jane Cowl or Julia Marlowe invested it. She had to utilize the equipment God gave her, not to falsify Shakespeare's creation, but to realize a different facet of it."[2]

Dramatic vision consists of actions imaginatively conceived, and language does not describe events in environments with sufficient precision to permit exact recovery by an interpreter. Even if, as in highly philosophical plays, the meaningful action is the juxtaposition of ideas, they take order from a structure of physical action whose details of movement, costume, and environment are explicated neither by the dialogue of classic plays nor by the gratuitous descriptions of a Shaw or a James M. Barrie. Gaston Baty wrote: "A text cannot say everything. It can only go as far as all words go. Beyond them begins another zone, a zone of mystery, of silence, which one calls the atmosphere, the ambience, the climate, as you wish. It is that which it is the work of the director to express."[3]

The director of a *written* play creates, must invariably create, from the concepts engendered by the script. The play director's vision, based on his analysis of the script, becomes the informing vision, and he, not the playwright, must fix the form of performance so as to express the vision he holds.

Some, like Fermin Gĕmier and Baty, may have bent this privilege to their own advantage, justifying their personal inventiveness as an expression of the impalpable values they discovered within the script's language. Possibly however, criticism of them derived from a reluctance by literati to accept the conclusions we must make about the relationship of the director to the playwright or the script: a workable playwright-director relationship depends upon an honest understanding that the artwork is the performance, and that its form is determined by the artistic vision — derived from whatever source — held by whoever supervises that performance.

2. Ibid., p. 16.

3. Quoted by Helen Krich Chinoy, "The Emergence of the Director," in *Directing the Play,* Toby Cole and Helen Krich Chinoy, eds. (Indianapolis: The Bobbs-Merrill Co., 1953), p. 63.

Varying patterns evoke unique moods.

Note that when possible I have avoided using the conventional word *playwright* to describe the one who conceives and *director* to describe the one who supervises the production. If language continues to be the chief medium of expression, these terms may endure. But I repeat that the theatre is a mechanism for organizing stimuli, *not essentially for the delivery of language.* Eventually we will develop creators who express their vision directly in theatrical terms. Why continue the conception, language, reconception, expression process by which purity is lost at every step?

For the present, however, when I say that the artwork is the performance and that the form is controlled by the performance supervisor's vision, I refer to the contemporary theatre director. He is the one, presumably, who studies the expressive powers of the theatre complex.

The writer should commend this assignment of responsibility, for it encourages the playwright to create theatre art, not literary art; to develop mastery of the theatre complex sufficient to direct the expression of his vision in its intended form — performance; or willingly to delegate authority to one having that ability, knowing as he does so that his delegate must, by natural law, express his own vision conceived from the script. Because he understands the implications of whichever choice he makes, the writer will not impede his director's expression by imposing such unreasonably rigid requirements that his executive cannot achieve their joint aim — the expression of the vision.

The director of another's playscript must acknowledge, in turn, that his purpose is to discover and express, not to refract the informing concept. Each word has a purpose, presumably, and he will modify a script minimally and only for artistic purpose — the purpose which he believes to be the playwright's. Once accepted, this division of responsibility will serve, but it depends upon the premise that twentieth-century theatre is an art-medium manipulated by the creator to control audience perception. By means of it he expresses his own artistic vision, whether derived from his or another's experience or language.

There is no intent here to expunge language from the theatre. My aim is to expand our creative use of the theatre-complex — to create, in addition to language drama, artistic theatrical experiences made possible by a new appreciation of, and way of using, the modern theatre's media.

These achievements are overdue. There is no merit in the tradition that theatre art is conceptualized by one and realized by another. Indeed, theatre, music, and dance are the only arts that distinguish conception from expression; and the dancer and the jazz musician, years ago, created new art forms by repudiating that tradition. Today folk-rock music and modern dance are possibly the most vital, dynamic, and significant arts of our age precisely because they are conceived and created by the same person. They are so complex that sometimes they cannot be written or scored; they are created by musicians who "show" each other what they hear. Application of this principle to theatre will be equally valuable.

*Everything important in art
happens at the very beginning.*

PICASSO

THE CONCEPTION

Racine's *Phaedra,* University of Iowa. Lael J. Woodbury, director; A. S. Gillette, designer.

3

RECONCEIVING
"WHAT SHOULD BE" —
THE PLAYWRIGHT'S VISION

The technique of reconceiving the playwright's vision is not the essential substance of this book. But because production principles apply universally to one's own or to another's conception, the following point of view is useful.

I said earlier that the director of a *written play* must invariably make concrete the concept engendered by the script. Regrettably, that statement is too generous. In my experience many directors see the script as an independent art object whose meaning is so clear that it need not be formally conceptualized, even by its director. In fact, they give little thought to a concept of the play, and are often inarticulate about it. They read it once or twice and then begin immediately to cast, block, and rehearse it.

But the text is never sufficiently specific to resolve the myriad choices the director must make. He — or his technicians — must choose atmosphere, colors, actors, qualities, and movements. And these decisions should be informed by the director's conception of the play. From the beginning it becomes the standard from which all judgments are made. As Oscar Hammerstein has said: "Most musicals are made in the first five minutes."[1] For once the conception is defined, other decisions derive from it.

When choosing one actor before another, a gray setting rather than brown, when costuming in rigid rather than soft fabrics, the director makes those choices that express his view of the play's meaning. That meaning is the conception — the grand view, the informing vision, the commanding metaphor, the central idea the play expresses.

Defining that conception, that metaphor, can be a tedious and hazardous procedure. Helpful techniques for arriving at or determining a master metaphor for a play have been usefully described by Mordecai Gorelik[2] and by James H. Clay and Daniel

---

1. Hal Prince, *Contradictions* (New York: Dodd, Mead & Company, 1974), p. 52.

2. "The Scenic Imagination," *Theatre Arts,* 40 (April, 1956); "The Setting And The Stage," *Drama Survey,* 2 (Winter, 1963); "The Scenic Imagination: 20 Years After," *Players Magazine* 42 (December, 1966); "The Scenic Imagination: Still Evolving," *Players Magazine* 43 (October-November, 1967).

Krempel.[3] Jean Louis Barrault sees *Carmen* as a metaphorical bullfight. The Broadway stage production of *Angel Street* was created by its director in *cinematic form*. And Orson Welles's Caribbean setting for a production of *Macbeth* is well known. I see Racine's *Phaedra* as a sexual confrontation in an arena — a fact that generates a creative scenic and movement design.

Oedipus Rex, for example, poses a number of troublesome production questions. In the opening scene the village elders have assembled before the palace entrance because the king has spiritual as well as political power. "You are not of the immortal gods, we know," says the priest. "Yet we have come to you to make our prayer / As to the man surest in mortal ways / And wisest in the ways of God."

But contemporary audiences find little spiritual authority in today's kings, and none in palaces as sacred places. How shall the director convey the spiritual needs which assembled the chorus members and made them see Oedipus as their only relief? How can he express to an audience of populists the awe with which the chorus regarded their king? Even more troublesome, how can he generate in the audience a correct perception of Teiresias, a diviner, a seer, half prophet and half priest?

Shall the chorus or the actors wear masks? Why? Not because ancient actors presumably wore them. Surely that is the least justifiable of all reasons, however often cited.

A severely difficult problem for any director of *Oedipus* is devising the appropriate, justified movement for the chorus. Perhaps the original chorus did dance to the left during the strophes, and to the right during the antistrophes. But that rationale has no meaning now; in translation the odes lose those characteristics, and audiences are uninformed about the convention. Indeed, why must the chorus dance or move at all? Troubled priests and elders do not dance before palaces or churches in our society. There is no merit in or

---

3. James H. Clay and Daniel Krempel, *The Theatrical Image* (New York: McGraw Hill Book Co., 1967).

The *Oedipus Cycle*. Brigham Young University.

justification for the effeminate group posturing sometimes seen in today's productions of Greek tragedy.

Each director will choose for himself his answers to those questions. For me, they are accessible if I conceive of the play's people as an American Indian society. I would not reveal that concept to my actors. Such an image would confuse them. In addition, the audience would never know the device I used to resolve the issues of the play. But I envision the performance area as a sacred ritual arena or dance ground where the village citizens have come to perform actions, in appropriate accoutrements, which they have found pleasing to their gods.

Oedipus is the chief, a warrior who in the past defended them heroically, and who is personally capable of solving problems by virtue of his personal strength and valor — not only because he knows how to solve riddles! (That conception would also guide my suggestions to the actor about stance, movement, and attitude.) And Teiresias is a maker of medicine, holding precisely those spiritual qualities that the Greek Teiresias held. He not only knows the future, he, to some extent, makes the future. So when Oedipus abuses him, everyone knows that he will pay well for his intemperance.

The chorus's movement? The assembled group for generations has executed liturgical patterns, it came to this sacred place precisely to perform a movement ritual, it is attired for that purpose; so strong movement configurations are inevitable and come easily to mind.

So, too, do the answers to other production questions. I would not ask the designer for an Indian ritual arena, but I would request a partially circular acting area having surrounding elevations from which to enter and observe. Because I envision an arena of earth and rocks, I would suggest that the setting consist of broken, diagonal lines painted in earth-hues.

By continuing this process of measuring decisions against a master image, the director achieves artistic unity. The technique is a valuable strategy for selecting appropriately expressive elements with which to make the abstract conception concrete. It is the playwright's vision only as thoughtfully and selflessly determined by the director. But in the playwright's absence, it is an instrument that serves well.

Die Soldaten. From Jarka Burion's *Scenography of Josef Svoboda.* Wesleyan University Press, 1971.

34

4
CONCEIVING "WHAT IS" — PERSONAL VISION

Chapter three recommended a master metaphor or unifying image as an instrument for guiding a director's decisions as he makes a script concrete on stage. In that process, the director devotes his technique to the ideal of a synthesized work of art (*Gesamtkunstwerk*). Characteristically, all of its parts are proportioned by the vision of one master creator — the playwright, or, in his absence or abdication, the director. Symphonic composers, too, practice this aesthetic as they create for orchestral expression a score of privately conceived sounds.

Synthesis of parts, then, is one effective creative method. But we can, with equal merit, separate or splinter the artistic elements. Ideas, emotions, the dimensions of time, space, occasion, facility, the known predilections of contributing artists, all offer creative substance. Unity then derives from excellence of parts, rather than from subordination to a single concept. And by elevating all constructs to artistic levels, to their maximum beauty, we enjoy them for what they are, not for what they mean to become. Often in such art the aesthetic aim is not an illusion of synthesis, but the demonstration of the aesthetic properties of potential constructs of art.

If, for example, we decorate a room to display a painting to advantage, all aesthetic decisions derive from the painting, and the total visual effect is an illusion of synthesis, one perfect composition from which nothing may be taken or added without diminution.

But if we invite designers of furniture, of drapery, rugs, lamps, and ceramics each to place in a room examples of their finest work, given the conditions, perhaps, of a known color scheme, the results can be as elegant and harmonious as the rooms and buildings decorated by early Renaissance artists who worked under a similar method — an aesthetic wherein each creator demonstrated his independent artistic capability. To medieval men, their work was an expression of their devotion to God, for they saw in their birth as artists, and in their ability to create, a divine manifestation of their place in the Great Chain of Being. Inasmuch as their work measured their respect for God, art, even for the Medieval and early Renaissance contributing artist, had to be perfect in each of its parts even if only God saw it. It was not designed merely for its contributory value to the final artwork. Each part — even if placed so high in a room or on a building that its details were not apparent from the ground — each part was an independent art-object, possessing as much aesthetic value when closely examined as the whole to which it contributed.

The contemporary jazz musician practices the splintered aesthetic. Where symphonic composers subordinate the individuality of the orchestra's instruments to the grand sound of the ensemble, the jazz musician, uniquely appreciative of his instruments' expressive potential, improvises music demonstrative of his and its artistic competence. Whether soloing, collaborating, or supporting others' flights, his method is to retain artistic and instrumental individuality — working directly from vision to expression.

Jazz as an artistic innovation has a theatrical counterpart. I reasoned in chapter two that the theatre is, essentially, an art machine, and that its artwork is the performance. This machine can be likened as art instrument to the language of the writer, the clay of the sculptor, or the sounds of the composer. Presumably the theatre director, master of this instrument, knows more of its expressive capabilities than any other person. He knows its actual parts, knows how to use them, knows their effects. Better than the playwright he knows the aesthetic possibilities of light, color, space design, and especially the creativity of the actor and how to use and encourage it. He is potentially capable of controlling the audience's emotional response, so flexible are his means. He can require spectators — not merely urge them, but require them — to see precisely what he wants seen, and no more: a hand, a photograph (as in *The Glass Menagerie*), a pair of scissors (as in *Dial M For Murder*). In brief, the theatre with its turntables, its mechanically moveable floor sections, its electronic light and sound equipment, and the skills of its technicians, can literally control, in large measure, the sensory perception of its audience. And the master of this instrument can create artworks which only he can conceive by virtue of unique knowledge of his medium.

Traditionally, to make the play concrete, to express its meaning through actors, costumes, movement, light, and speech (the communicative media of the theatre) is the director's task. He searches the dialogue for clues to its values and relationships, then tries to objectify them. He may devise an elaborate metaphor, or select a "spine" of action, as an objective correlative of the play's meaning. Alan Schneider saw in the verbal thrust and counter of *Who's Afraid of Virginia Woolf* a contest, a game of chess, and he designed movement patterns which externalized in action the play's larger conflicts of spirit. Harold Clurman saw the search "to get connected" as the main action in *The Member of The Wedding.* That physical-spiritual objective pulled his Frankie — and his production — forward from scene to scene.

The director's practice of expressing meaning concretely is seldom challenged. If the director may move logically from meaning to concrete metaphor or objective correlative, then stimuli must within themselves contain decipherable meanings. If a director specifies a leap as a manifestation of joy, for him the sensation of joy must be at least inherent in leaps. This conclusion in no way inhibits the practice of leaping to express other, antithetical emotions, for actions are at least as ambiguous as words. But unless the director's practice of making meaning concrete is fraudulent, each emotion an action can express is inherent each time the action is performed within the same context.

So if the director can express meaning through concrete stimuli, meaning must abide in them. And because he is not a playwright, or dancer, but a director who works with it, he must be uncommonly sensitive to the stimulus-meaning relationship. He may, therefore, appraise what *is,* the stimulus, in search of its meaning or its experience content, and then create, as other artists do, a focused, proportioned, artistic statement in theatrical terms of the values he discovers there.

No longer reconceptualizing language to define another's vision of experience as described in chapter three, he creates for others a concrete, theatrical statement derived directly from his *own* sensitive

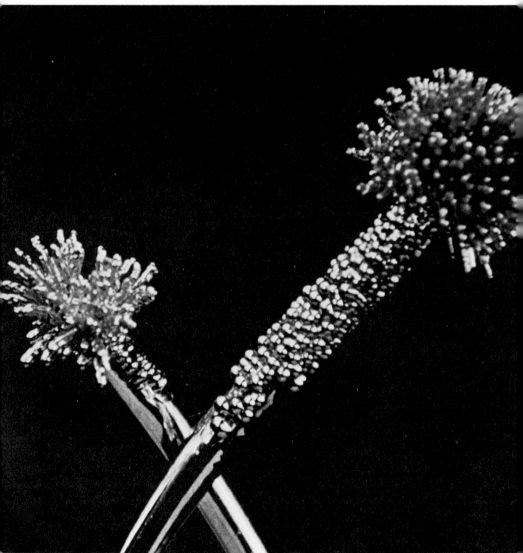

Electrochemical copper "flowers."

perception of experience. His product may or may not be theatre complex, as language-drama sometimes is not. It is a direct and concrete expression of what a single theatre creator derived from experience. His practice is not unlike the sculptor's, who looks at marble, decides what it contains, and eliminates irrelevant matter; or the musician's, who concludes that a clarinet best expresses certain music and then renders it; or the painter's, who creates a painting expressive of one color's values.

To demonstrate that stimuli such as visual images have meaning, which, when properly understood can be structured into concepts, V. I. Pudovkin intercut film segments showing a chess champion engaged in a match with film depicting two other people. By juxtaposition of these originally unrelated images Pudovkin produced a story, Chess Fever, actively involving all three, although the chess player had no thought, at the time he was photographed, of the others who performed with him in the edited story.

The Cool World, a film documenting the condition of the Harlem Negro, apparently evolved, in part, from stimuli-cinematic improvisations. It is built from seemingly random shots of Harlem: tenements, store fronts, passersby, buses, trains, dogs, playgrounds, and people. When spliced into the basic story, such images, having meaning, must influence and shape the final story, substantially determining the conception of the film.

In theatre and cinema's conventional practice, we write the story, specify the images needed, then set about to find or make them. But here, instead of ordering "Here is the story, express it with images," we ask, "Here are the images, what story do they tell?" The final product expresses not what ought to be (the playwright's vision), but what is (the film images).

These examples derive from cinema. In theatre the theory that an artistic statement can be developed from actors' improvisations is not controversial. Evidently A Hatful of Rain by Michael V. Gazzo owes its inception to improvised scenes. But this method of creating theatre art is not widely practiced. And why should it be? Why require actors to create for the playwright? After all, the intended art-object remains the same — a language-drama. It is in no way superior to or different from a conventional drama. Besides, improvisations are an uneconomical way to create plays. Why use a group of actors to do in concert what a writer can do alone?

Suppose, however, that we reject all preconceptions of our artwork and simply ask ourselves: "Here are the theatre's media; what do they mean?" Follow, for a moment at least, the practice of sculptor Len Lye. "Art is emotion," he says. "I'm not representing or conceptualizing; I'm expressing. I get the compulsion to make something; then I pick up anything around — paper, wood, wire, metal — and hook it up to see if it makes anything significant to me. [I try to 'discover' a new form that expresses] my *feeling* about the universe — not a representation of the universe itself."[1]

Choose a single stimulus, a sound, for example — a high, thin sound of some duration. It is the sound composers often select to express tension, the quality of waiting expectantly, as when one pauses before a door, unsure of whether to enter. Its quality can be varied to evoke apprehension or resignation, but now it is the high, thin sound produced by a single violin string. What feelings, what images does it suggest? It is a simple, a lonely sound. Because it does not expand it seems to diminish. It suggests a cry, a faint voiced searching, perhaps an echoed keening or unspeakable yearning. It pulls the listener forward, engaging him, leading him, coaxing him forward.

The sound is not an experience-equivalent, it is a direct experience. It has no verbal equivalent; it is what it is — a simple sound to which we respond differently and according to our mood. Once determining its quality, we can illustrate, explore, or amplify that quality with other media. We can create an atmosphere in color, people the stage with actors moving in actions expressive of the mood, and erect structures which give the actors interesting movement areas while conveying emotions by space relationships. We can explore each aspect of the sound-experience — thin, high, lonely — in

---

1. "Timehenge," *Newsweek*, 22 March 1965, p. 94.

Meaning as forms.

Meaning as forms.

sequence, taking needed time, repeating for emphasis or contrast, or juxtaposing qualities in sequence or in concert. And it is a simple matter to enrich the sound by varying its resonance, instrumental source, amplitude, or its pitch. But then the sound might be described as music.

The parallel is meaningful. The function of the dancer, according to the philosophy epitomized by the choreography of George Balanchine, is to express the essence of abstract musical sounds in movement. It is not the story of music (as in conventional ballet) which such movement expresses; the aim is to depict in pure movement the immediate experience of music. True, interpreting music in movement is not unlike interpreting a script in speech and action. But music is a direct sensory experience, while a script is a description (or prescription) of experience. The choreographer determines the significance of a sensory experience (not music invariably — it might be sound, gesture, or color, for example) and expresses artistically in other stimuli that significance as understood. Merc Cunningham, for example, sometimes rubs balloons together creating a sound. He then dances the sound — or expresses in movement what the sounds mean to him. (In a parallel technique, Japanese actors may enact *emotions,* rather than the *actions* which preoccupy Western actors.) The virtue of this practice is that the choreographer's art work, inspired by direct experience, is expressed immediately as experience through media indigenous to the theatre by one uniquely qualified to do so. The difference between a *danced interpretation of musical sound* and a *danced story accompanied by music* emphasizes the distinction.

Sound is experience which can be expressed theatrically. The emotional and intellectual values of other stimuli — light and color, or space, mass, form, and line — provide additional artistic matter. We may create theatre sculptures, massive constructions which only theatres can house, and display the unparalleled beauty of large, complex masses moving under imaginatively conceived light. An abstract structure revolving on a theatre stage, planes and levels formed by light before the beholder's eye, mysterious masses

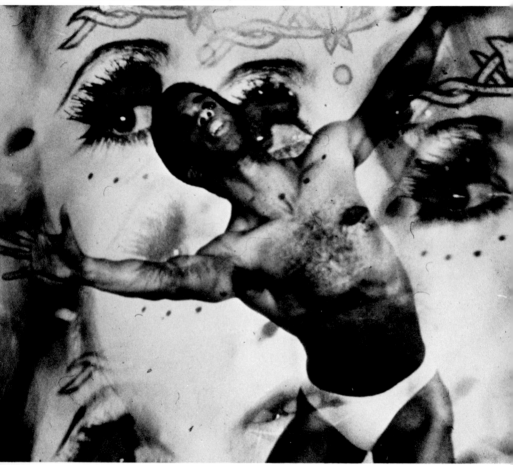

Meaning as form and movement.

splitting and meshing, skeletal forms suspended in awesome tension between beams of shimmering blue and green will bring audiences to an appreciative hush. These are not idealistic generalizations. We have seen prototypes of such sculptures in the stage settings for *Oliver, The Music Man,* and many university productions.

And there is aesthetic justification for depicting constructions in the theatre as art works — unless one can envision only language-drama on the stage. One of the distinctive aesthetic experiences theatre provides is plastic movement, and, as Mr. Lye has said, movement must have space. "I don't give a damn for gallery shows," he remarked. "My things ought to be shown in scale, as a huge vibrating steel symphony on the desert floor of Death Valley, or as a 'Timehenge' in the Tennessee burial-mound country — twelve pieces, perhaps 150 feet high, in a circle, like England's druidical Stonehenge. I work with movement, and movement must have space."[2] The theatre provides appropriate space for massive sculptures, for it can present them ideally while rigidly controlling the audience's perception.

Theatre sculptures are not less artful than conventional sculptures. Conceived with an acute appreciation of light and color and a sense of dramatic tension, they express the artist's perception of beauty in form where others see only things. Sculptors and graphic artists ponder beauty in "found" objects: driftwood, a cut stone, a chain, a bicycle, a painted board, the wheel from a tricycle. Micro-photography reveals the beauty of a fly's eye, of a watch mechanism, of a snow flake. Indeed, the popularity of "Happenings" reflects an interest in experiencing the "now," the inexplicable beauty of a moving figure on roller skates, an undulating flag, fireworks, paint splattering from a dripping faucet, a recording of traffic sounds, or a man-figure walking, running, kneeling, leaning, or swaying. Unlike the graphic arts, however, the theatre also reveals form sequentially in much the same way a movie camera explores for thirty minutes a

2. Ibid.

45

masterful painting — communicating a profound sense of the whole by minutely examining and comparing its parts.

It is noteworthy that when Western students study the fundamentals of composition, they select a square of paper (never a round) and sketch on it an arrangement of elements which satisfies the basic principles of design — balance, tension, rhythm, unity, emphasis. The student learns by so doing that composition is a process of organizing, form imposed upon element, a product mainly of reason. In Japan, however, students of composition analyze a photograph, print, or drawing, and then scissor the reproduction into smaller interesting and expressive compositions. By so doing they learn that composition is not necessarily a structuring of beauty, but beauty discovered, form found, a triumph of perception, not only organization.

When the eye tires of the stage sculpture, new tensions can be introduced by commenting upon and embellishing a composition with light and color. Theories exist about the emotional significance of light and color; now demonstrate their worth. Create a light dance, a composition of varying color and intensity, of course, one having divergent thermal qualities, one where light explodes, burns, throbs, and shimmers. Can light modulated by music or sound evoke emotional response? Place on a turntable a construction of parallels, platform tops, ramps, and a high flight of risers. Revolve it under general blue light, then under over-head intense magenta, then under brilliant red from a high upstage-center spotlight, as though backlighted. The light will dance the set to life when it creeps over a platform, hurries to another, tentatively approaches the steps, and then rushes up to them to leap beyond our view. It becomes, if artfully done, a *theatre symphony,* having a beginning, a middle, a climax, and an end — an exciting sensuous experience expressing another's experience and artistic judgment. Someday, hopefully, we will manipulate visible light beams to suggest forests, skyscrapers, and abstract forces; or we will design exciting visual patterns having no expressible purpose beyond the interest of their composition.

In summary, audiences will delight in the theatre sculpture we

Potassium dichromate crystals in anti-freeze solutions.

Theatre sculpture piece, *Midsummer Night's Dream*. Tomlinson Theatre, Temple University. Joel Friedman, director; Daniel Boylen, designer.

envision if, having created it artfully, we reveal it artfully. We will manipulate it to present each of its parts, then articulate them to demonstrate their action and relationships. We will evoke mood by washing the scene or segments of it in the abundant colors and qualities of light which we control. We will emphasize interesting aspects of its structure — independent compositions — by pinpointing artful segments with tightly controlled light.

We more than double our expressive means when we place man on this ever-changing sculpture, complex though their aesthetic relationship is. Adolphe Appia contemplates that relationship in his *Work of Living Art,* and *Man Is The Measure Of All Things.*[3] There he describes how the time-arts of poetry and music coalesce with the space-arts of design and plastic form through the actor's revealed movement. He extends his analysis to describe how man animates plastic form, how in our context, theatre sculptures can be animated by actors or dancers moving among or on them.

At the Theatre of the Bauhaus, the man-plastic form relationship was illuminated by a series of production experiments.[4] Where playwrights traditionally structure a human action (an action of men in conflict), by which means their psychology, their social and environmental relationships are manifest, the Theatre of the Bauhaus explored the aesthetic implications of man as form only. For man is more than ego, more than personality, more than a social creature. He is a remarkable machine, and man as machine can function artfully. As architecture he displaces, gives form to, space. Man moves not only volitionally but in reaction to rhythm, objects, and the movements of others. Man is transcendental form. Art depicting these qualities expands the actor's role. Like sound and sculpture, the experience of which can be explored artistically, man as form generates unlimited substance for creativity. For example, I have

---

3. Adolph Appia, *Work of Living Art* and *Man Is the Measure of All Things,* trans. H. D. Albright (Coral Gables: University of Miami Press, 1960).

4. Walter Gropius, ed., *The Theatre of the Bauhaus* (Middletown, Conn.: Wesleyan University Press, 1961).

described choreographed movement directly expressive of the sound of sound. But sound is not movement's only possible impetus; a master of movement, sensitive to its meaning, will find creative material in man's gesture and action. "It is the dancer that suggests the dance to me," says Balanchine, and when he creates from this source he is not expressing music spatially.[5] He is expressing in action action's meaning — meaning derived only from action.

This important procedure is not comparable to the director's conventional statement that he learns from watching his actors which directions to give them. Then he is interpreting the script, fundamentally, and he analyzes his actors to discover how they express the script most believably. But when we express action's meaning in action we need no script or music; we create, not from an informing vision conceived by another, but from actual experience.

If, for clarity's sake, we gesture to convey meaning, presumably meaning — informational, aesthetic, or both — is implicit in a cocked wrist, a flexed knee, an extended arm. There is artistic substance in widespread hands, an arching sweep of the body, a dragging foot, a short hop, an S line of movement, a searching for equilibrium, successive or appositional lines in the human figure. There is meaning in an extended stretch, a converging pattern of action, a double somersault. If we place actors who move well in a space having various levels and ask them to move about easily, to and away from each other, we discover in their changing relationship the genesis of experience which can be refined into a significant artistic statement.

We may perceive there emotional relationships indicative of elaborate physical actions. We may make concrete in movement and a design of figures such feeling-states as hunger, love, fear, hate. This art is not precisely dance as conventionally defined. The actors are constructs of briefly static human art-objects designed to objectify the emotion that inspired them.

---

5. "Lark from Russia," *Newsweek*, 15 February 1965, p. 87.

Man as architecture.

Man as design.

Or ask an actor to move, then present him with objects to which he must adjust. An actor empty handed, one dribbling a basketball, and another carrying a mandolin, behave differently, even when they mime their burdens. Their action can be analyzed, proportioned, and integrated into a design that derives directly from how they adjust to their objects. Their performance may have no meaning to which we can give a name, but the movement of their bodies under light, the unique articulation of their animated figures, their personal rhythms, the juxtaposition of their actions, individualized or synthesized by the objects which they manipulate, unquestionably can be artful.

Or ask actors to improvise a sequence involving physical contact. Their inventiveness can charge an observer's creativity. If the meaning of *Who's Afraid of Virginia Woolf* can be expressed artfully by conceiving the action pattern as a gigantic game of chess, if the spiritual values of Racine's *Phaedra* can be made concrete by designing movement from the image of a confrontation in an arena, surely the reverse may be true, wherein actors' movements are refined to express the spiritual content inherent in movement's nature.

Thus action's perceived meaning can be expressed as pure or abstract action, or as pantomime expressive of an emotion, an ideal, or a story. Whatever the product, the aim has been constant: to discover the meanings of the stimuli which the theatre controls, and, having discovered them, to structure them into an artistic statement indigenous to the theatre complex. From immediate experience the director creates art experience which he presents in experience form.

This type of theatre differs from traditional drama where story is the framework of the play's substance. Ordinarily story is a chronologically developed conflict which is resolved after a number of reversals and complications. It is revealed as a carefully calculated series of events, each proportioned to the story's needs. While movement, lighting, and the constructions I have described also can be structured into story-telling relationships, they are closer in kind to contemporary forms of drama.

In the cinematic spirit of depicting rather than describing the action or the play's meaning, many new plays are ingenuously

concrete. If men cannot communicate, provide the actors with
nonsense words or sounds; bury a woman in sand if she is mired in
the world. Alfred Jarry's Pere Ubu (in *Ubu Roi*) is clearly gross
because he, the figure we see, is almost entirely belly. His grossness
is not implied, it is explicit. The metaphorical substance of such
plays often has more meaning than their language. Indeed, the
language may merely reinforce the concrete metaphor of the action
— a theatrical experience depending for effect primarily upon stimuli
other than language.

Unlike chronological drama, today's theatre experience, whether
conceived by director or playwright, often reveals panoramically. It
does not reveal man through an analysis of how he responds to
conflict; it presents a cycle of experience — explicit, concrete
experiences usually revolving about a central idea, memory, or
emotion. *The Chairs* by Eugene Ionesco, depicts two people in an
empty world, waiting for company, for instruction, for meaning. But
to convey that meaning Ionesco posits a panorama of experiences
illustrating moments in their lives. Freed from the laws of
chronological consistency they relive, discuss, and demonstrate
acts and conversations which sharply define the central and simple
point of the play: the "nothingness" of their (or our) existence. The
play's form is cyclic, a collage. It is unified, not by development of
character nor by the resolution of a dramatic question, but by the
point which the segments of the play illustrate.

Incidentally, the creative director can, if he sees it, make a positive
statement about the worth of man and his world. He can show what
man and his surroundings actually are, not what they have been or
are thought to be. Beauty abides in the elements if not the whole of
any structure. It exists in color, light, shadow, and their relationship.
And it exists in the human figure. If we cannot *write* in our age about
man's grace, dignity, and virtue or form, we can express those
qualities visually.

Of course, the spoken language of *The Chairs* is an important part
of its substance. I have withheld comment on speech in this chapter
in order to stress the importance of analyzing experience and

conveying it concretely — to emphasize the truth of Max Beerbohm's observation: "Television [and theatre] is not literature, it is actuality." Teachers of improvisation know how difficult it is for actors merely to study and react to each other. Actors insist upon launching immediately into a contrived dialogue. Invariably they assume that theatre is language and that they must talk.

However, if language contributes to the communication of experience, the creative director will use it freely toward an art of theatre that is uniquely theatrical, that derives from all the materials of theatre. By adopting an inverse creative method, by analyzing what the theatre complex is, not what it might be, the director will derive his own statement. It may be as brief as the illumination of a theatre sculpture, man or object; or a combination of sound, movement, and light that evokes the qualities perceived in sound or other stimuli. It may be structured into a chronological development of character and story, or it may be formed into a cyclic representation of experience pertinent to a central concept. Language may or may not carry part of its burden of communication.

Suppose, for example, that while observing actors we are impressed by a recurring action: perhaps a suggestion of physical or even spiritual rivalry, perhaps a quality of sexual conflict. Perhaps we become most interested in the simple actuality of the converging of two human figures. This image invariably suggests a rich and intensified relationship, whether the figures converge in order to destroy, to caress, to ignore, or to dominate.

Indeed, the experience of coming together is common; it underlies much human activity. As a theme it can be explored by every theatrical means: light encountering light, color meeting color, form against form, man meeting man, or myriad and complex combinations of these. And each encounter can be modulated by varying the quality of its expressive elements. What are the aesthetic implications of red against orange, blue against green, male against female, curves against angles, curve against red against blue? Here is unlimited artistic substance.

But conventional audiences are most interested in human

encounter. If we find interest and stimulation in two converging figures, we and the actors together can explore the innumerable ways in which human figures come together. They can walk toward each other, to be sure, although they may creep, rush, limp, fall, dance, or leap as they approach. But what happens after they meet? Do they stop and peer? Do they avert gaze and avoid? Do they touch, walk around, or keep their backs to each other as they glide past? What happens when two figures touch, and how do they touch; with a handshake, a grasp of the forearms, with one hand or two? Suppose two figures face, lift both hands high and lock them. Is there a quality there of union — or conflict? If they lean forward in thrust position, hands locked high above them, are they straining toward or away from the encounter?

From *Encounter* a two-hour aesthetic experience can be fabricated. A director might demonstrate how parts of a construction encounter, how light and color meet with constructions, how color acts upon color, aural rhythm upon visual rhythm, and, of course, how man encounters any or all of these. Whether the director explores or reveals the experience of forces meeting in other media, he can devise an almost conventional theatrical experience from the actor's movement, from speech, and from his and their response to what they see and know. What is said then derives from the director's (or actor's) personal interpretation of *what happens* as the actors move. Speech here is not redundant because the purpose is to convey, not exclusively to dance, the experience. Speech heightens the expression, enriching the texture of encounter in the same way that costumes, lights, and music do. Speech, then, if used, is often improvised. Or, if not improvised, it is carefully selected after the experience to be explored has been identified, and it derives directly from exploration of that experience.

The text of such a performance — less specific than a scenario — has most meaning for those who conceived it, for it is a scant reminder of what they have done or concluded, not a prescription for what they should do. But for illustrative purposes the following example is based upon familiar quotations: Orpheus retrieving

Ambivalent encounter. Unconventional theatre, Brigham Young University.

Eurydice from Hell (Ovid, *Metamorphosis,* Book X); Romeo meeting Juliet (Act I, Scene 5); Jacob wrestling with the Angel at the river Jabbok (Genesis 32:24–32); and Brer Rabbit sticking to the Tar-Baby (Joel Chandler Harris, *The Complete Uncle Remus,* Story 2).[6] The substance of this encounter-collage is its movement, the action of coming together which is common to each of the four stories. The movement is the performance's essence. It inspired the theme and conveys it directly, and it reinforces the four stories — told simultaneously — which, in turn, accompany and enrich the action. Such movement is more complex, subtle, and extended than words can describe.

The experience of movement and these quotations reflect the ambivalence — the simultaneous fascination and horror — of many encounters. For union requires subordination of individuality; both rapport and conflict lie at its base. Orpheus, braving Hell's tortures for his love, loses her in a gesture of tenderness. Romeo and Juliet find love through combat, a competition of wit. Jacob resists attack, defends himself from his own creator, and, because he fights valiantly, is blessed and loved. And when Brer Rabbit seeks love and fights for it, he sticks fast to his opponent.

The rapport-conflict paradox is emphasized by juxtaposing the four stories. By viewing the action and hearing the quotations, the audience is forced to an awareness of ambivalence as a common quality of human experience — encounter — which unifies the action. Of course, for performance the theme would be further explicated by additional theatrical media — music, light, costumes, and an acting area, expressive of mood, which complemented the movement design.

Envision, then, an acting area complicated by a variety of cubes and squares suggesting an abandoned quarry or a canned-goods warehouse strewn with weight-supporting boxes. A rough, irregular crescent of independent screens defines the area. Each screen is

---

6. Suggested by Roger Pierce.

coarse-textured and of muted color, and each revolves intermittently on its vertical axis as though stirred by an unfriendly wind. Void exists beyond the screens. Descending from the blackness above is a weathered, perhaps suspended, flight of steps. The FIRST actor appears at the top of the stairs, pauses, and says simply:

  And Jacob was left alone.

 Actor TWO has mounted a screen's upstage side and now it revolves and presents her (or him) to the stage as she says:

  Orpheus mourned her to the upper world,
  and then,
  Lest he should leave the shades untried,
  Dared to descend to Styx. (She steps out).

ONE: (Descending)
  Gods of the world below the world, to whom
  All of us mortals come, I come
  For my wife's sake.

(From some distance they regard each other. They start — a circular pattern. Negotiating the obstacles, they move, revolve completely, mount and dismount the cubes.)

  I wanted to be able
  To bear this; (coming together)
  I have tried to.

(In profile, in deep positions, they extend arms, reaching strongly, one placing his palm up, another down, until their palms touch lightly, as ONE continues:

  Love has conquered.

(ONE grasps TWO'S hand, gives a mighty jerk lifting TWO through the air in a gymnast's somersault. TWO lands on a cube behind ONE and while ONE dances or shuffles around him, TWO dances something like a waltz-clog while she tells the audience:)

  Brer Fox went ter wuk en got im some tar, en
  mix it wid some turkentime, en fix up a
  contrapshun
  w'at he call a Tar-Baby, en he tuk dish yer
  Tar- Baby en he sot-er in de big road.

Bimeby
her come Brer Rabbit pacin' down de road,
dez ez sassy ez a jay-bird. He fotch up on
    his
behime legs like he wuz 'stonished.
ONE: (Circling with fascinated attraction) Mawnin!
    Nice wedder dis mawnin. How you come on, Den?
    Is you deaf? Kase if you is, I kin holler
       louder.
(Whirling away, navigating the obstacles:)
    By these places
    All full of fear, by this immense confusion,
    By this vast kingdom's silences, I beg you,
(TWO steps down, participates in an action counterpoint, ends
action on opposite side of stage from ONE.)
    Weave again Eurydice's life, run through too soon.
TWO: They called her,
(Long pause — both to each other, maximum awareness of the
other).
    Eurydice.
(starting together — an exaggerated limping, danced encounter)
    She was there, limping a little
    From her late wound,
    With the new shades of (their hands touch)
    Hell.
ONE: (Seizing TWO'S hand)
    You er stuck up, dat's w'at you is,
(ONE flips TWO through somersault as before)
    'en I'm gwine ter kyor you,
    dat's w'at I'm a gwin ter do.
(TWO flips ONE in a similar manner. One hand of each remains
engaged through the following movement, but the action is slow now
and stylized as in a Balinese dance — perhaps in slow motion or as
under water.)
ONE: And there wrestled one with Jacob until the

breaking of the day.

(With a hand of each engaged, the actors now change mood and explore the possibilities of strong movement in their relationship. With strength but with dignity and grace they pivot, turn, pull away, wrestle, push, revolve under one another's arm, and in effect create a two-figure space dance.)

TWO: Brer Rabbit keep on axin' im, en de Tar-Baby,
She keep on sayin' nothin, twel presently
Brer Rabbit draw back wid his fis', he did,
en blip he tuck 'er side er de head. Right
yar's whar he broke his morlasses jug. His
fis' stuck, en he can't pull loose. De tar
wilt 'em. But Tar-Baby, she stay still.

(With a distinct change of quality, the actors shift their grasp until only a palm of each is touching. Again an action, but now sensually, as the actors gently explore a ritual of love. The actors need not always stand; they may sit or lie. The palm contact is everpresent but not blatant. It is incidental to the fact of two persons wanting each other near. Perhaps they dance, even waltz: they flee, pursue, stretch, almost break the bond, then turn and pivot inward until secure within the arms of the other. There is time for this. The substance of the moment is the action of the figures, not the dialogue.)

ONE: If I profane with my unworthiest hand
This holy shrine, the gentle sin is this,
My lips, two blushing pilgrims, ready stand
To smooth that rough touch with a tender kiss.

TWO: Good Pilgrim, you do wrong your hand too
    much,
Which mannerly devotion shows in this,
For saints have hands that pilgrims' hands
    do touch,
And palm to palm is holy palmer's kiss.

ONE: (The mood changes:)

Ef you don't lemme loose, I'll know
you again.

TWO: En wid dat he fotch 'er a swipe wid de
udder han', en dat
stuck.

(ONE attempts to strike TWO, they both join both hands, and they mime the action of trying first to conquer, then to free themselves. But the quality of the struggle changes gradually from that of the Tar-Baby encounter to a more serious, meaningful struggle. Within minutes the image changes from two tenuously joined figures to a more compact mass possessing internal struggle. The actors are now on the floor in classic wrestling position, and their combat is slow, ritualistic, and in deadly earnest. Finally, while both are prone, ONE locks TWO's left arm between his feet, and stretches TWO's right arm taut with his hands. There is a pause while he applies immense pressure, then ONE says, demanding surrender:)
And the Angel said to Jacob:

TWO: (Resisting, but almost faint from his effort)
Let me go, for the day breaketh.

ONE: I will not let thee go, except thou bless me.

(More pressure. A pause. They test each other. Then TWO nods agreement, ONE releases her. They take time to breathe, to gather strength, to recover.)

TWO: What is thy name?

(She moves above him, ONE is seated. TWO places a hand upon ONE'S head, raises the other hand high and circles ONE during her speech of blessing.)

ONE: Jacob

TWO: Thy name shall be called no more Jacob,
but Israel; (raising him)
For as a prince hast thou power with God
and
With men, and hast prevailed.

(They have been touching, but now TWO, still reaching to touch, backs away and starts to glide slowly among the screens. ONE

follows part way, yearning to touch, to feel, to maintain contact.
TWO moves in an arc upstage of him, and ONE follows with his gaze
and attention, still reaching.)

ONE: Tell me, I pray thee, thy name.

TWO: (Retreating) Wherefore is it that thou dost
        ask after my name?

ONE: (Following TWO part way, ONE mounts a cube for
        spiritual power.)
        my only love sprung from my only hate.

(ONE pauses, twists away, begins line, and starts up the steps
part way.)
        Prodigious birth of love it is to me
        That I must love a loathed enemy.

(On the steps, turning, a new quality)

TWO: (Moving out onto acting area, studying the area, the
        cubes, the earth, the heavens, then facing front:)
        For he had seen God face to face, and his
        life was preserved.

ONE: (who has come to the foot of the steps on ONE'S last
        speech)
        Orpheus climbed the upward path, through
        absolute silence.
        (He begins mounting the steps.)
        Up the steep murk, clouded in pitch
           darkness,

(TWO racing around the crescent of the screens, spinning them
— they have revolved intermittently during the entire performance —
and speaking the lines. She is, at the end of her lines, at the base of
the steps, reaching, yearning, repeating in the line of her body the
general configuration of the steps.)

TWO: They were near the margin, near the upper
        land,
        When he, afraid that she might falter,
        eager to see her,
        Looked back in love, and she was gone, in

a moment.

(The screens swing, TWO pauses for a moment, then starts to move off among them, into darkness.)

ONE: He could hardly hear her calling,

TWO: (as from a great distance)
             Farewell! (pause)

ONE: When she was gone.

(TWO is off, ONE, yearning to advance, retreats up the last steps. The screens paw quietly at the void, as darkness gathers the scene.)

God Is In The Details.

MIES VAN DER ROHE

THE EXPRESSION

Tension in form and meaning.

5
TENSION

The director selects and proportions sensory stimuli either to convey what he reconceptualized from another's vision, or to express his own. The two methods are not antagonistic, for in both cases the director's media are stimuli that he manages for artistic effect. With his media he brings the audience to a measurably predetermined response. Therefore, I will not henceforth distinguish between the director's conceiving and reconceiving; for his aim, the aim of all artists, is constant: to express a vision so as to affect the perceptor in a reasonably predictable way. The following chapters discuss in detail, first generally, and then specifically, how the theatre's stimuli generate response.

That which holds our attention determines our action. Contemporary plays often pose a metaphor, and "hold our attention," by unfolding the metaphor's construction. Traditional drama, however, depicts man in conflict — a conflict which structures the play's plot, characterization, language, spectacle, and philosophy. Will Oedipus identify the person responsible for Thebe's curse? Will Hamlet destroy Claudius? The posing of such conflicts induces tensions which, cyclicly, intensify the conflict and require audience response. In his preface to *Arms and the Man*, G. B. Shaw wrote: "Every drama is the artistic presentation of a conflict. The end may be reconciliation or destruction, or, as in life itself, there may be no end; but the conflict is indispensable: no conflict, no drama."

Therefore, tension, or its planned absence, is a general artistic factor properly pervading every element of artistic expression. The dramatic question or conflict may itself carry the burden of holding the spectator. Or the means of expressing the question can be so manipulated that they generate a condition of tension among stimuli which complements and intensifies the drama's conflict. Because drama's conflict in plot and characters is designed by the playwright and because tension within expressive media (such as form, space, and mass) is designed by the director, we may say that what conflict is to the playwright, tension is to the director.

Tension should not be confused with suspense. Their meanings are similar, but not identical. Suspense suggests a waiting, an inanimate state, a pause without an end (from *suspens,* delay, deferring). Tension suggests *forces in conflict,* rivalry, power, pressure, and resistance (from *tendere,* stretched tight, strained, taut). Thus deliberate tension exists in every artful work — even those, such as painting, that ordinarily do not use suspense as a technique — for tension heightens perception.

Tension derives from an inhibited or arrested tendency — a condition demanding catharsis. We know tension in life when we encounter jeopardy but cannot, for some reason, act against it. The tensions developed by the inhibition of our response endure until danger passes or until we are distracted by larger problems. Perhaps such tensions never expire; perhaps they diffuse into the subconscious. We ignore them, we surrender to them, or possibly, we direct defensive aggression against what we mistakenly imagine the cause of fear to be.

Because it issues from an inhibited tendency, tension in life is usually viewed as a negative condition. Art, however, exploits its positive significance. Art consistently makes a statement that activates a tendency, a response, next inhibits that tendency, and then provides a significant and calculated resolution to the tension it generated. Curiously, this artificial risk or frustration, intolerable in life, is pleasurable in art. Art induces tension an audience can interrupt at will by leaving the artwork, but it waits for resolution seemingly in pleasure proportionate to the tension's magnitude. (Furthermore, tension tends to narrow one's awareness to the tension-producing experience — an important artistic principle.)[1]

Dancer Doris Humphrey writes: "My entire technique consists of the development of the process of falling away from and returning to equilibrium." She finds this fall an "exciting danger," the recovery

---

1. Aldous Huxley, "History of Tension," *Annals of the New York Academy of Sciences,* ed. Otto v. St. Whitelock, vol. 67 (New York: The Academy, 1956–57).

from which is "repose and peace."[2] The merit of this technique in graphic art is confirmed by Gyorgy Kepes: "The internal forces constitute the dynamic tendency of the individual to restore balance after each disturbance from the outside [whether from art or from life] and to keep his system in relative stability. . . . We cannot bear chaos — the disturbance of equilibrium in the field of experience."[3]

The artistic process consists, then, whether in music, painting, plotmaking, or in the director's manipulation of the theatre's media, of inducing a tendency which is then complicated, contrasted, or contradicted by another's artistic thrust. In the theatre, in addition to traditional dramas that generate tension by posing a conflict, a dramatic question, and usually by depicting within the plot the conflict between what is and what should be, a director may also construct artful and compelling tensions within those means — light, sound, movement, composition, and others with which he makes his vision concrete.

I can illustrate the principle most clearly on these pages through visual examples. These drawings also make use of the principle of emphasis, but they demonstrate that controlled tension, because tension engages interest and conveys meaning, is a useful directorial technique for manipulating audience perception. To express the point another way, the sound of a gasoline engine lacks significance, interest, or meaning. But if we interrupt or inhibit that aural statement periodically, we monitor tendencies, we induce tension, we create meaning sufficient to produce emotional, intellectual, and physiological responses.

The principles expressed in these drawings can be applied directly to the stage, for any object placed on the stage, like any object placed on canvas, enters into a relationship with all other objects within the field of vision.

2. "My Approach To The Modern Dance," in *Dance: A Basic Educational Technique,* ed. Frederick Rand Rogers (New York: MacMillan Co., 1941), p. 189.

3. *Language of Vision* (Chicago: Paul Theobald and Co., 1959), pp. 16, 31.

Tension can be created among lines by means of contrast in direction, length, shape, and width.

Direction	Length	Shape	Width

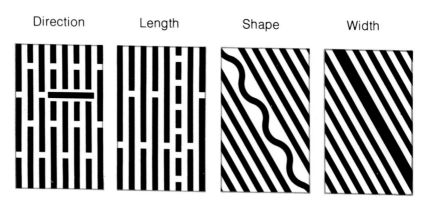

Tension can be created by offsetting balance or equilibrium and by playing complementary directions, lengths, and general characteristics against each other. Skillful combinations of these principles produce line rhythm.

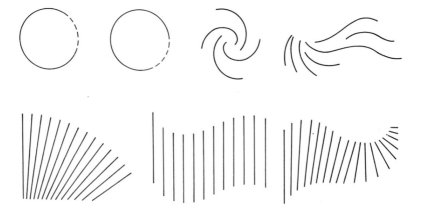

Color tension can be created by manipulating value, hue, and chroma.

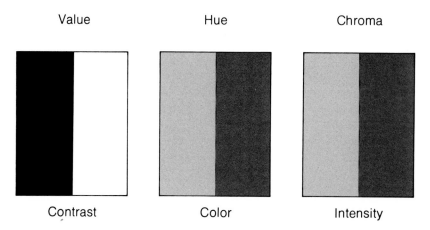

Value	Hue	Chroma
Contrast	Color	Intensity

Tension can be created in space: size, shape, and distance.

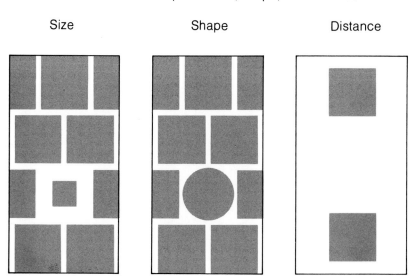

Size	Shape	Distance

Tension can be created between surface planes and axes.

Between Surface Plane

Between Axes

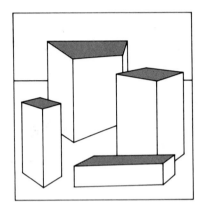 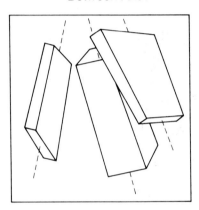

Tension can be created between textures.

Polyekran. From Jarka Burion's *Scenography of Josef Svoboda.* Wesleyan University Press, 1971.

Indeed, all of the sensory elements of theatre can be transformed into tension-bearing relationships by placing them in opposition.

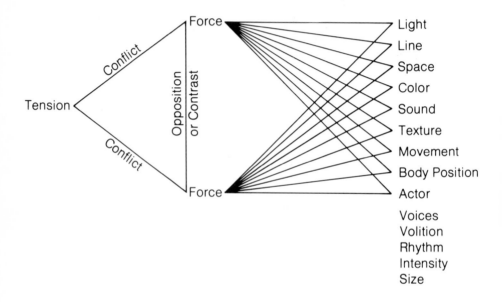

When art posits a tendency (a stimulus) that is manipulated by the artist so as to engage the perceptor physically and psychologically, the resultant tension contributes in two ways to the art experience: as the product of an inhibited tendency it provokes the perceptor to expect a condition of equilibrium, thus engaging this attention and analytical faculties; and, hopefully, the artistic concept is conveyed by the nature of the tension established. For example, the elaborate apparel in Claudius's court visually establishes a mood or quality violated only by Hamlet's "inky cloak." The ensuing color tension compels interest, of course, but it also conveys pertinent intellectual and emotional values. The director's objective, then, is to generate tension among the stimuli he selects for expressing his vision.

To achieve this aim the director may exploit the fact that each phenomenon in the universe exerts its own dynamic force. This statement is true of every line, color, taste, form, temperature, and quality. Each phenomenon exerts such power, and resists ingesting the force of another. If it did not resist, all distinction of parts would disappear, and each quality or thing would consume another before being itself consumed. Visual verification of this statement abides in the illustrations offered earlier, or in the tension created in this tendency — ////// — by introducing axial tipping — /////////////// or

in the tension we perceive when light strikes any object. A universe without objects is black. We do not see light without objects, or objects without light. What we witness is the collision between light and obstacle.

The Duke of Saxe-Meiningen, who carefully analyzed the laws of tension observed by graphic artists, systematically pitted the forces inherent within the form of proscenium arch (a line tendency) against the force exerted by the form of his settings (the inhibition). He designed so that the setting's rear wall line did not parallel the line of the proscenium opening. He specified step units which had three, five, or other uneven numbers of risers. Conscious of the tensions within visual elements, he observed:

1. It rarely works to have a figure dead center.
2. Two actors should avoid standing in similar relation to the prompter's box.
3. All parallels on the stage are to be avoided as much as possible.
4. A single person, facing the footlights squarely, is bad.
5. An actor should not move in a parallel [straight] line.
6. If three or more actors play a scene together, they should never be placed in a straight line. They must stand at angles to each other. The space between the individual actors must always be uneven.[4]

Another common and effective technique introduces "time tension" by interspersing an accelerating and extended dialogue with pauses of unpredictable frequency and length, demanding and focusing audience attention where desired. Peter Brooks exploits this technique when he counsels performers of Shakespeare to avoid general rhythms — to express individual rhythmic patterns of speech that will give their characterizations distinction and will subtly emphasize their emotional estrangement.[5]

Emotional tension is often heightened by artful actors who take care that their emotional spectrum in performance is unlike any other's. By omitting emotional transitions they contrast the extremes of rapture and despair. More easily, they reduce their emotional level to a point just below those about them. Sometimes, but not often, such crafty performers exaggerate their emotional intensity, but they then run the risk of seeming forced and insincere. Whatever their technique, however, they induce a tension that distinguishes their performance.

Sergei Eisenstein introduced a single element, related motion,

4. Quoted by Max Grube, *Geschichte der Meininger;* reprinted in *Directing The Play,* ed. Toby Cole and H. K. Chinoy (Indianapolis: Bobbs-Merrill Company, 1953), pp. 71–78.

5. Charles Marowitz, "Lear Log," *Tulane Drama Review* 8 (Winter, 1963): 103–21.

and then a tension-producing association that heightened intellectual and emotional response. The results were remarkable. In his montage list for *Strike*,[6] for example, he specified scenes showing the killing of workers intercut with shots of the butchering of a bull — the latter being the associative element. The same technique can be applied in the theatre by means of projections on cycloramas and screens, of course, although the principle of the associative element has a wider application.

Color tension, too, or its absence, provides substance for the technique. The use of two primary colors of equal and intense saturation prevents one from gaining dominance. The effect of contriving a setting out of squares of blue on a red background would be to inhibit audience stability, possibly even disorienting it because of the absence of any point of focus.

Obviously, too, one might choose for effect those colors which, when placed in juxtaposition, create a throbbing, shimmering, or pulsing effect within the spectator. That these effects could be programmed for an entire evening is doubtful, but there may be plays, scenes, or moments when nothing else would communicate the desired effect so well.

Perhaps the most sophisticated and useful technique consists of establishing a condition of tension by *contrasting what we show with what we know*. In *The Bald Soprano*, for example, we deduce from the actors' behavior two couples who have met for refreshments and conversation. But the text we hear is largely unintelligible. Ionesco brilliantly compels our attention until we share his conclusion that typical conversation is meaningless, after which there is no point in continuing the play. It is obvious why plays of that genre are usually presented in one act.

Cinema (e.g., *RACHEL, rachel*) exploits this same principle when it introduces a fast or slow motion (the final scene in *Bonnie and Clyde*). A standard of lifelike tempo is established, after which the standard is deliberately accelerated or retarded. Our urge to

---

6. *Film Form*, Appendix III (New York: Harcourt, Brace and Co., 1949), p. 57.

perpetuate the realistic tempo, newly violated, generates the tension that makes the scene compelling.

The ballet dancer does what we know he cannot do — leap and remain suspended. Graphic artists, too, deliberately contrast what is known with what can be seen. Some, such as Toulouse-Lautrec and, perhaps, Michelangelo, limned figures which, in one pose, represented sequential points of time. That is, when depicting a figure in action, the representation would, at various points of the body, show the wrist at one moment in the execution of the action, the arms as seen a moment later, the head as seen still a moment later, and so on through the body. The technique, of course, projects a quality of contained energy, of movement, of action. The one illustration, through artful use of tension, gives the spectator the experience of a complete action.

Indeed, the psychological power of tension is so valuable that it has been used to generate even false perceptions — to make the unreal real. A former inmate of a Chinese Communist prison affirmed tension's irresistible force when she described her experience there. The Chinese had been "absolutely justified" in arresting her for her "acts inimical to the Chinese people," she said. She had been chained and handcuffed at intervals for several months. "I was handcuffed and had ankle chains," she stated. "I did not consider this as torture. They use chains to make you think seriously about things. It could be described as a form of punishment for intellectual dishonesty. *The main thing about a Communist prison is that it is a place of hope. . . .*" (London *Times,* 1 November 1955.)

Her tension was compelling, and its effect upon her was profound. Created by pitting the force of confinement against the tendency of freedom, her condition was so acute it introverted her perception, inverted her values, and made her pathetically appreciative of the fact of her own imprisonment.

Thus we see that tension is a formidable instrument. Whether created by emotional or physical stress or by artful frustration, a condition of tension generates favorable conditions for perception.

Atmospheric rhythms. Wagner's "Die Walkure."

6

SURPRISE —
ABSTRACTION —
DISTORTION —
REPETITION —
ATMOSPHERE

Tension is fundamental to all art. A universal quality, it monitors the meaning of any stimuli we organize. Later we will consider the artistic use in theatre of individual stimuli. But there are, in addition to tension, other universal principles that affect audience response.

Trite stimuli do not stimulate. This fact is insufficiently appreciated. Even astonishing theatrical pieces such as the elaborate melodramas of Dion Boucicault in the nineteenth century pale after audiences anticipate their content.

Therefore we can be sure that current modes of theatre will be different a few years hence. After the Civil War in America, styles began to change at twenty-five year intervals; during the mid-twentieth century they began to change every eight to twelve years. They shift so rapidly now that many styles exist side by side. Of course, this eclecticism constitutes a style of its own.

It is noteworthy, then, that all art that endures — that has a truly artistic dimension — contains an element of freshness or surprise, a unique perception of form or content that gives it distinction and compels the attention of an audience. An artist is wise to ask himself not only, "Is what I have to say significant?" but, "Am I saying it in a fresh way?"

I once watched an interesting director work with a young performer in *The Mouse Trap*. The actor was creating a conventional and believable character, and I was willing at the time to accept his achievement. But the director said to him, in effect, "What you are doing is adequate, but there is no distinctive quality about it. It's the kind of performance given by any reasonably capable actor anywhere." The actor argued that his only responsibility was to create the character that Agatha Christie had written, and I was inclined to agree with him. But the director did not. He maintained "You can do better." When the actor asked how, the director replied, "Just make this character interesting." The actor at first was without ideas, but he eventually performed with a new attitude and style which made his characterization singularly artful.

My point here is that the artist created a beautiful and fresh performance because he was directed to do just that. It was an achievement of reason. He consciously set about to give unpredictable dimensions to his performance, and by so doing he elevated it to the level of art. This principle is apparent in every great artwork — the unexpected musical interval, the whispered rather than the predictably shouted phrase, blurred rather than crystalline cinematography, actors who fly as well as run.

A corollary of the artist's search for freshness is that his work continues to satisfy only so long as it continues to feed. That is, the quality of art is measurable by its ability to withstand an audience's tendency to tire of it. This principle directly repudiates the traditional concept of clarity in art. It derives from the observation that without exception great art in every mode has an ambiguous quality, and it is that ambiguity that arrests man's inclination to pass it by. Ambiguity perpetuates interest. *Othello* is a lesser play than *Hamlet* because there is more to learn about Hamlet, his perceptions, and his values and motives. *Electra* is a lesser play than *Oedipus* for the same reason.

This generalization means that an art piece must have a degree of complexity in order to be art. The comic strips' Prince Valiant and Flash Gordon are well drawn in terms of movement and composition. But they are cartoons by definition because they lack profundity. We only glance at them before reading their dialogue. Norman Rockwell's paintings share the same criticism.

Another universal artistic principle is that of abstraction, although theatre, because of its traditional content, is slow to adopt its use. Music, of course, consists of absolute abstractions — sounds in time devoid of connotations of human relationships. The statement that art does not mean but is is nowhere truer than of music. Thus music might serve as a model for an acceptable abstract theatre. Wagner, Appia, Meyerhold, and Tairov believed that it could. But when we depart from Aristotle's dictum that tragic drama is the depiction of human action, we immediately hear: "Yes, but what does it mean?"

To abstract, in my view, means to reduce an art object to its essential design. An abstracted skyscraper might consist of a vertical line; the abstraction of a flower might be a splash of purple. Since I here am preoccupied with the fundamental constructs of theatre, I envision our working almost exclusively with them as abstract elements. We try to see them not only for what they mean but for what they are. Enough was said about this technique in chapter four that it need not be embellished here. But the process of arranging abstract elements so that they constitute a new abstraction is a valid artistic practice.

When rearranging abstract elements we should give special attention to the principle of distortion. Distortion energizes objects so that they acquire life. Moholy-Nagy in *Vision and Motion* holds that distortion equals motion (because distortion expresses the discrepancy between the way a thing should appear and the way it actually does appear).[1] A rhombus is an existing geometric shape. Yet, when we view it, it is difficult to believe that what we see is not a square about to snap back in a moment into its proper form. Thus when shapes or characterizations are given subtle distortion they can either enhance or explode the unity of a work.

Henri Bergson applies the statement, "Distortion is a normality which needs to readjust itself or snap back," to the comic play. A distorted person loses his humanity and becomes an object, and we laugh at the effect:

The comic is that side of a person which reveals his likeness to a thing, that aspect of human events which through its peculiar inelasticity, conveys the impression of pure mechanism, of automatism, of movement without life. Consequently it expresses an individual or collective imperfection which calls for an immediate corrective.[2]

Thus we correct the distortion within the comic frame by laughing.

Two factors to watch when distorting for emotional effect are these: 1) Deviations used repeatedly become norms. When this happens, it is necessary to invent new deviations for the sake of emotional impact or to emphasize those already in use. 2) Distortions that cannot be related to the standard of that which is human have little emotional effect. More accurately, they create their own effect independent from that which the artist originally distorted. According to Rudolph Arnheim:

---

1. Moholy-Nagy, *Vision and Motion* (Chicago: Hillison & Etten Co., 1947), p. 118.
2. Henri Bergson, "Laughter," in *Comedy* (Garden City, New York: Doubleday & Co., 1956), p. 117.

In the representational arts the distortional effect of certain shapes is again enhanced by the notions of normal shape the spectator has formed through experiencing his memory. . . . There are, however, limits beyond which the frame of reference will not stretch. It is probable that for many a beholder the flagpole-shaped figures of the sculptor Giancometti or the obese nudes of Lachaise are not fully relatable to the human body; these figures appear as creatures of their own kind. . . .[3]

I look upon this tendency to apprehend distortion freshly as a singular virtue. Marshall McLuhan argues that junkyards, whether of ideas, machines, or values, are an inspiration to the artist because in junkyards constructional elements are no longer seen as parts of a whole but as the individual constructs they are. Consequently, the artist sees them anew and devises means of constructing new ideas or art objects never before conceived. Picasso, as well as notably the surrealists and other disciples of the "Found Object" movement, found ways, sometimes for comic effect, of making art objects out of discarded bicycle handbars and automobile parts.

Consequently, distortion is valuable for helping us see not only man and his action but also to see abstract elements (such as the vertical line of his body) which constitute his essential design.

Still another artistic element to be considered is that of repetition. Bergson has observed that repetition, as well as distortion, introduces mechanical qualities having comic potential.[4] He notes that in life no gestures, no movements, no ideas, are exactly alike and that when we repeat any stimulus regularly we begin to anticipate its repetition so as to notice it and to be amused when we see it appear.

Bergson refines his idea into this generalization, "In a comic repetition of words we generally find two terms: a repressed feeling which goes off like a spring, and an idea that delights in repressing the feeling anew."[5]

But Susan Langer relates the effect of repetition to the fulfillment

---

3. Rudolph Arnheim, *Art and Visual Perception* (Berkeley: University of California Press, 1954), p. 348.

4. Bergson, p. 81.

5. Ibid., p. 107.

THIS FIGURE WAS PRODUCED BY DR. FREDERIC I. PARKE, UNIVERSITY
OF UTAH COMPUTER SCIENCE DEPARTMENT, AND SUPPORTED BY THE ADVANCED
RESEARCH PROJECTS AGENCY OF THE DEPARTMENT OF DEFENSE UNDER
CONTRACT NO. DAHC15-73-C-0363 AND CONTRACT NO. F30602-70-C-0300.

The common made uncommon — computer art.

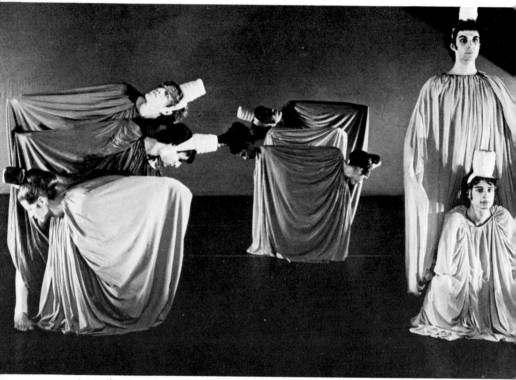

Intensification through repetition and release.

of expectation or the release of tension. She explains that a baby laughs at a toy that is made to appear suddenly again and again because his wish is gratified, the suspense is broken, and his energy is released.[6]

In *Concerning The Spiritual in Art* Wassilly Kandinsky observed that repetition is a means of intensifying and communicating the ambience surrounding all artistic statement.

Repetition . . . thickens the spiritual milieu that is necessary for the maturing of the finest feelings, in the same way that the warm air of a greenhouse is necessary for the ripening of fruit. An example of this is the case of the individual who receives a powerful impression from constantly repeated actions, thoughts, or feelings although singly they might have passed unnoticed.[7]

So convinced was Kandinsky that the ambience pertinent to art could be composed, intensified, and communicated that he envisioned a "monumental art" which would coordinate and unify the different art media available to us.

In this art among innumerable rich and varied combinations at least one is based on firm fact and is as follows: The same internal tone may be achieved by the different arts; each art will bring to this general tone its own special characteristics thereby adding to it a richness and a power which no one art form could achieve. The immense possibilities of profundity and strength to be gained by combination or by discord between the various arts may be easily realized.[8]

Wagner organized this spiritual plasma into leitmotifs or musical identities for characters in his musical dramas. That is, his music suggests or conveys a spiritual quality unique to each character — a quality preceding and perpetually radiating from him.

---

6. Susan Langer, *Feeling and Form* (New York: Charles Scribner's Sons, 1953), p. 340.

7. Wassilly Kandinsky, *Concerning the Spiritual in Art* (New York: George Wittenborn, 1912), p. 65.

8. Ibid., p. 64.

Composer Leonard B. Meyer observes that repetition generates a new meaning transcending that communicated by the original statement.[9] He notes that the repetition or seeming repetition of a part arouses more specific expectations than the first statement and that one must be careful to give an expected variety and to try to fulfill the expectations repetition generates.

And Kandinsky tries to explain the nature of those expectations:

The apt use of a word in its poetical sense, its repetition, twice, three times, or even more frequently, according to the need of the poem, will not only tend to intensify the internal structure but will also bring out unsuspected spiritual properties in the word itself. Further, frequent repetition of a word (a favorite game of children, forgotten in later life) deprives a word of its external reference. Similarly, this symbolic reference of a designated object tends to be forgotten and only the sound is retained. We hear this pure sound, unconsciously perhaps, in relation to the concrete or immaterial object. But in the later case pure sound exercises a direct impression on the soul. The soul attains to an objectless vibration, even more complicated, I might say more transcendent, than the reverberation released by the sound of a bell, a stringed instrument, or a fallen board. In this direction lie great possibilities for the literature of the future. . . . An ostensibly neutral word in its felt quality will become somber as Maeterlinck uses it. A familiar word like "hair" used in a certain way intensifies an atmosphere of sorrow or despair.[10]

A principle that can inform the manipulation of all stimuli for predetermined purposes derives from the artful control of atmosphere. A general mood or atmosphere pervades every script, and it is the director's responsibility to discover and define this atmosphere and to choose communicative media with the single thought of emphasizing and expressing it. This was the technique described in chapter three in which the director polled his sensory response to the

---

9. Leonard B. Meyer, *Emotion and Meaning in Music* (Chicago: The University of Chicago Press, 1956), p. 49.

10. Kandinsky, p. 34.

play and then used those responses as guides to the selection of expressive media.

There are, however, substantially broader aspects of atmosphere. The theatrical experience begins at least as early as the first perception of advertising the producer selects for promotion of a play. We often know from the graphic design of the play's title whether to expect comedy, tragedy, or naughty farce. And so a predisposition towards the event begins no later than that moment. And this conditioning continues through all the additional contacts the spectator has with the production until he is seated in the auditorium and the curtain is open. Then, of course, the performance itself and its atmosphere affect him.

But much can be done about conveying an atmosphere for favorable perception prior to the performance. In my view Max Reinhardt gave more useful thought and has written more about this matter than any other. In traditional theatre an artistic objective is to create an impression that something significant and interesting is about to occur. Reinhardt began generating his "festival effect" by recognizing that each play, because of its unique atmosphere, requires a special place in which to present it. Therefore he was careful to mount plays only in theatres — large or small — that he thought appropriate for them. He used a square in front of a cathedral for an open-air *Everyman*. He mounted plays in the Grosses Shauspielhaus as well as in the Olympic Hall in which he constructed the image of a church with a stained glass window thrice the diameter of the Rose Window in Notre Dame. In addition, he produced in the Kammerspiele, an intimate theatre which he used for chamber plays.

A small hall without galleries and with stage scarcely separated from the auditorium, paneled in warm brown. In this hall, at the same time cozy and solemn, the lights are not extinguished suddenly, but there is a gradual passing from light to darkness. Thus everything in this little playhouse is calculated to prepare and maintain an atmosphere of concentration.[11]

11. Heinz Herald, "The Kammerspiele," in *Max Reinhardt and His Theatre*, ed. Oliver M. Sayler (New York: Brentano's, 1924), p. 147.

Reinhardt's practice of calling the audience from the dinnertable by means of trumpets and prayers expressed at strategic points throughout the city was laudable. In fact, the tendency toward expanding and exploiting the principle of preperformance atmosphere is continued by those producers of Shakespeare today who have their performers dance, sing, and sell presumably period confections such as horehound, tarts, and oranges before the production.

When Reinhardt's *The Miracle* audience entered the theatre it was led through the following sequence:

Flickering light from behind columns as invisible candles throw shadows, flags and lanterns in the auditorium, shafts of sunlight, windmachines, thunder drums, voices to be heard. Audience takes seats, everything is dark, soft candlelight in auditorium, only when necessary. Clusters of candles in distant places, in auditorium and stage, high up in tower, produce suggestion of tremendous size and distance. A praying voice is heard, chairs are pushed about, after that silence. The play begins.[12]

This summary of stage directions illustrates the pains Reinhardt took to ensure an appropriate atmosphere for the play.

A singular dimension of atmosphere is the effect temperature can have upon an audience. The story is told by the manager of a prominent popular singer about how he advanced her career. She began by singing in unknown bars and small night clubs. But as she acquired prominence it became apparent that each time she sang, the audience was uniquely stimulated to a new appreciation for her. "Why is it," her manager was asked, "that each time she comes on stage the audience stops drinking and smoking and gives its full attention to her — more than any other performer of the evening?" "It's very simple," he replied. "After the audience has been drinking for a while we have to compete for its attention. I just walk over to the thermostat and turn the air conditioning down as far as possible a

---

12. Max Reinhardt, "The Miracle," in *Max Reinhardt and His Theatre*, ed. Oliver M. Sayler (New York: Brentano's, 1924).

Abstracted visual elements.

few minutes before she enters. This clears the air, promotes circulation, and clears the minds of the audience."

This tactic may be only a trick, but I suggest that a director steep his mind with imaginative ways to manipulate response. Ultimately he is responsible for every perception of the audience, and he must monitor each sense as carefully as he does the positioning or costuming or lighting of the actor at the center of the stage.

Still another atmospheric dimension is generated by textures. Mexico taught me the rich suggestion of warmth and coolness texture can provide. Little use of shade or trees is made in Mexico. Small thick-walled houses bake in the sun. They have obviously been there for years; no one has designed shade around the house or yard. Yet Mexican people find effective comfort in a hot region. Their walls are often eighteen inches thick; their windows are small. The interiors of their homes are dark; and by use of color they suggest an inviting coolness. The textures they use are smooth, hard, and simple. For decoration they use glass, tile, hard wood, cement, and stone. Often they use wooden shutters rather than drapes, a choice emphasizing their predilection for hard smooth planes. They use few brocades or carpeting. And the result is that their buildings are attractive and comfortable.

Instead of relying solely upon gelatin color for the effect of heat as we do in such plays as *The Emperor Jones,* we could create a hotter atmosphere by more artfully selecting the textures we display. A common error when suggesting the coolness of a grotto is to fill the stage with greenery — flowers, trees, vines, bushes, shrubs — supposing that this mass of plastic vegetation will seem cool. The effect is quite the opposite. Because the scene is so busy and the texture so complex, the temperature seems to rise. The green color suggests coolness, but the texture works against that tendency.

On the other hand, a difficult quality to evoke on today's large stages is the feeling of a small room in which people actually live. Because the surfaces are broad and the planes are unbroken, because of so much wall and floor space, the audience acquires a sensation that the characters live in barnlike caverns. Thus the atmosphere such textures create works against the believability of the scene.

The production elements — surprise, abstraction, distortion, repetition, atmosphere — are found in varying degrees in all art. But they are singularly useful to the director who is structuring the abstract meanings he finds in theatrical stimuli into concrete artistic statements. Not only will he use them to give form to his expression, but his continual analysis of them will provide substance for additional artistic works.

Die Soldaten. From Jarka Burion's *Scenography of Josef Svoboda*. Wesleyan University Press, 1971

7
SPACE ORGANIZATION

Directors commonly believe that stage composition consists of placing actors in expressive positions, or in such a way that the audience will invariably see the point of greatest significance. They think it is the physical relationship between objects that creates right visual effects and that line, mass, and form are the essential components of the stage picture.

This misconception continues the popular belief, described in chapter four, that composition is an arranging process, a mixing of objects to create desired form. That view is encouraged by Alexander Dean's excellent text, *Fundamentals of Play Directing,* where he describes how to analyze visual emphasis, stability, sequence, and the emotional values of line, mass, and form as elements of stage composition. But despite my keen appreciation for Dean — his book is mandatory reading for any stage director — I believe it is more accurate, and more helpful, to view composition as the proper arrangement of space.

I once found an artist sitting on a stool throwing pieces of torn paper to the floor about him while studying the results intently. "What do you see," I asked, "the forms the paper makes?" "No," he replied, "the space the paper defines." The philosopher Lao-Tze said: "A vessel is useful only through its emptiness. It is the space opened in a wall that serves as a window."

The way space has been used or organized has changed during each of the ages of man, and each of these methods of organization is still available for our use according to the effect desired. Sometimes linear perspective is de-emphasized because customarily a neutral architectural unit serves as backing for a frieze of figures.

Or space is developed in units having equal iconographical and spatial significance. Neither space nor time is represented realistically.

This concept expanded during the Byzantine period into the *hieratic* system of perspective — a system that depicts what one knows rather than what one sees. Usually the compositional elements are reduced in size and grouped around a large, dominant

Trivulzio Ivory. *Landmarks of the World's Art.* Jean Lassus, 1967.

Frontispiece of the first Bible of Charles the Bald.

figure. There are generally three tiers on the surface plane of a painting of this style. Heaven occupies the top third, earth occupies the bottom third, and the subject of the painting fills the space between.

During the late medieval period (as early as Alberti — 1435), the concept of one-point or parallel perspective became important. Time in painting became frozen — represented only one moment — and space became important iconologically. This technique provides a finite expression of what the artist sees as a finite world. It focuses the eye, abruptly narrowing the spectator's view. It is characterized by sharp outlines and by a distinct arrangement of visual elements. Interestingly, Marshall McLuhan sees the beginning of one-point perspective as the beginning of individualism and of man's alienation from society.

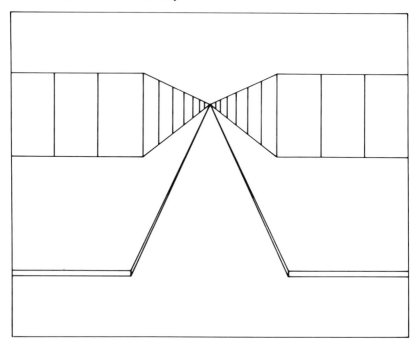

Parallel perspective is typical of the Renaissance, but angular perspective was adopted from the sixteenth century on to Cezanne. In angular perspective space expands with distance, and the main action is set back and related to a few forms in the foreground. The effect is that of opening a window upon a scene. Overlapping planes are easy to use here.

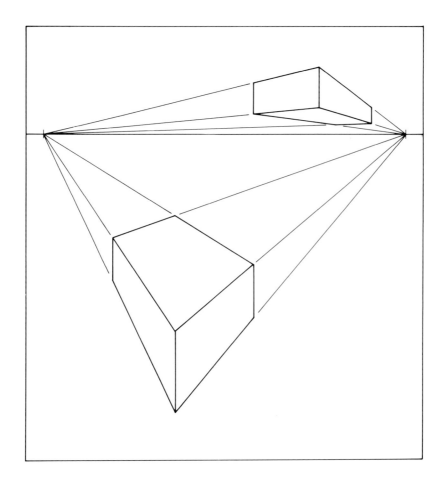

Today's practice is to depict no sharp outlines, and to let the iconological value of space succumb to an expression of the importance of space itself.

The Orient, uniquely, follows a technique known as the receding diagonal.

In a different categorization, a recurring concept of space organization is the primitive, in which we confine space to the surfaces of the artist's material. That is, we do not free space from the material in which we build. Another trend is the conceptual, in which the artist expresses an idea or an emotion. The illusion of reality is secondary here. Naturally there is an arbitrary handling of space, and distortion results from such freedom. A third method of space manipulation is empirical. Here the artist recreates what he observes. Here space is absolute, quite different from the primitive who depicts the surfaces of what he sees. Finally, there is a relativistic use of space in which no absolute reality exists. Space is an impersonal, constant flux. There is no single point of view. The viewer may or may not be in motion, and such space is validated by the individual observer. This is, of course, the kind of space manipulation favored by today's painters. Perhaps the best single example would be the paintings of Picasso in which he shows at one time three different views of the model's head.

It is helpful to view space, or, more accurately, to feel space as marble or clay to be molded and transformed. Space is a substantial object subject to the physical laws of movement, mass, and weight. We do not model space-mass by "poking holes in it" but by molding it around the already present holes in space that objects constitute.

Or we can see space as palpable motion constantly flowing around objects. In our context actors are the obstacles impeding the flow of space, thus forcing it to move around them, while space in turn encompasses the actors totally. In a sense, then, the actor is carried along by the motion of space as by a liquid stream. Whenever he resists the flow, he creates tension. Space itself changes the form of the actor; at the same time the actor influences the form of space.

In either image, space has substance. Thus the director has two phenomena with which to compose — space and objects, thesis and arsis, positive and negative substance. By systematic penetration of space with various stage objects, or the actor's body, the director creates a tension-experience. He places forces in opposition. Space pushes in, around, and upon the man-figure, and the figure resists with its own counter force. Chapter five explains how this tension gives vitality to the audience's perception of the mass of space and the mass of the figure.

It is important, here, to discuss what we know about what we see. The only generalizations we can make about the mechanics of seeing are these: the eye prefers to move horizontally; vertical eye movements are tiring; clear vision takes place only when the eye is fixed (it is temporarily blinded when in motion).

But perception, alone, is not seeing. According to Arnheim, all perceiving is also thinking, all reasoning is also intuition, all observation is also invention. . . . Vision is not a mechanical recording of elements but the grasping of significant structural patterns. . . . Every act of seeing is a visual judgment. Judgments are sometimes thought to be a monopoly of the intellect. But visual judgments are not contributions of the intellect, added after the seeing is done. They are immediate and indispensable ingredients of the act of seeing itself. Seeing that the disc lies off center is an intrinsic part of seeing it at all.[1]

Such visual judgments imply a process of organization. When we experience an image, we creatively integrate its elements. Like a musical chord we perceive its unique form while at the same time remaining aware of its component notes. Thus the elements of an image are more than the sum of their mass, for each element perceived generates an influence not unlike the magnetic rays surrounding objects having electrical energy, and these force fields interact with each other. They provoke a stress or pressure within the beholder that is potentially profound. For example:

Until you have felt that apparently infinite expansion of a French Gothic nave, while your physical being expands as though a new and wide world were opening about you, while your spirit grows in you and you feel enlarged into something finer and more able than you

------

1. Rudolf Arnheim, *Art and Visual Perception* (Berkeley: University of California Press, 1954), pp. viii ff.

thought was possible, you don't know what space means, and you don't know that in the XIIIth Century in France the world saw one of its greatest states of human development and capacity.[2]

The laws of inertia are as applicable to art as they are to physics. Each object retains its quality of force, movement, or form, until that quality is challenged by another quality. Thus a good space composition consists of a delicate balancing of forces that the eye tries to perpetuate. Light striking new elements within the composition alters that balance and thus generates perception and an awareness of tension or imbalance. "Any line drawn on a sheet of paper or the simplest form modeled from a piece of clay is like a rock thrown into a pond. It upsets response, it mobilizes space. Seeing is the perception of action."[3]

Or, as Kepes says:

The experiencing of every image is the result of an inner action between external physical forces and internal forces of the individual as he assimilates, orders, and molds external forces to his own measure. The external forces are light agents bombarding the eye and producing changes upon the retina. The internal forces constitute the dynamic tendency of the individual to restore balance after each disturbance from the outside and thus to keep his system in relative stability.[4]

We walk against the resistance of the earth; we fly buoyed up by the resistance of the air.

This resistance is powerful and real. As Appia pointed out, when a living figure approaches and touches a static object such as a pillar, the pillar is made to live; both objects relate to but resist each

---

2. Allen Tucker, *Design And The Idea* (Washington, D.C.: The American Federation of Arts, 1939), p. 20.

3. Arnheim, p. 5.

4. Gyorgy Kepes, *Language of Vision* (Chicago: Paul Theobald and Co., 1959), p. 16.

other. The same effect appears when we photograph a barren stairstep and then take a picture of the same step showing the foot of a man upon it. The practice of photographing a person in front of a cathedral does more than establish the relative size of the building. It animates the scene because their forces in opposition generate life.

Gyorgy Kepes suggests that we place a hand on a piece of paper and note how their complementary flat planes produce an inert composition.[5] But when either the hand or the paper is pressed or contracted the composition acquires a dynamic quality, for both exert strong fields of force that oppose but balance.

Richard G. Wiggin says: "The key force which accounts for our reacting to visual objects and sensing space between them, is induced by a 'pulling' or a tension created between them. . . . *Space is the result of the organization of tension created between objects or forces.*"[6]

Placing objects in space tension creates a plastic image, but for the image to persist as a structure, the relationships between objects must constantly change. Change implies motion. Otherwise perception decays. The eye must move from one stimulus to another in order to generate an impression of plasticity.

Surprisingly then, a space composition must have a time as well as a space dimension in order to sustain a response. The same is true of sound, of course. Sound is a time medium, obviously. It can be perceived only in time. But to the eye space is time, and therefore plastic images well perceived can be said to have a time structure.

Thus it is that artistic space organization consists of appropriate recognition of the dynamic forces surrounding objects in space, the lines of force space itself exerts upon them, and the aesthetic use which may be made of both.

Artistic organization gives the beholder both pleasure and

5. *Ibid.,* p. 36.

6. Richard G. Wiggin, *Composing In Space* (Bloomington, Illinois: McKnight and McKnight, 1954), p. 13.

meaning. As Japanese calligraphy conveys text while evoking delight in form, so too will space and objects when artfully juxtaposed. The objective of the artistic director is, in an aesthetic manner, to lead the eye through the composition in the exact sequence and with the exact result intended.

As an initial referent he composes visual elements in relation to the frame of his optical field — the proscenium, usually, or the stage floor if the auditorium is sharply raked. As we have learned, seeing is the perception of relationships, not merely the perception of units. There are no absolute qualities of light, color, or form. Elements

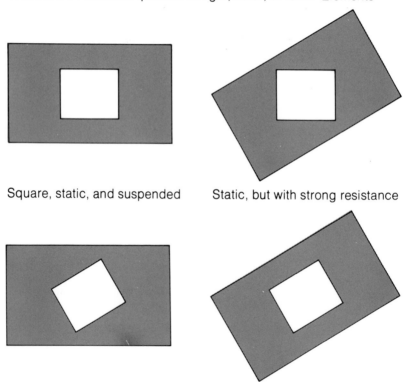

Square, static, and suspended   Static, but with strong resistance

Without stability — less concrete   With the potential of movement derive their qualities from their relationship to all objects in view. These diagrams taken from Kopferman illustrate how the quality of a rectangle is altered by changing its relationship to its border or frame.[7]

It is possible, at this point, to decide whether the stage picture will restrict or liberate the spectator's gaze. If, as is easy and common, the director sees up-center-stage as the point of emphasis, he is thinking of the stage in terms of one-point or parallel perspective. Here the dimension defined by the proscenium arch constitutes the front plane of the space cube, and the viewer sees through that plane to a converging point at its rear.

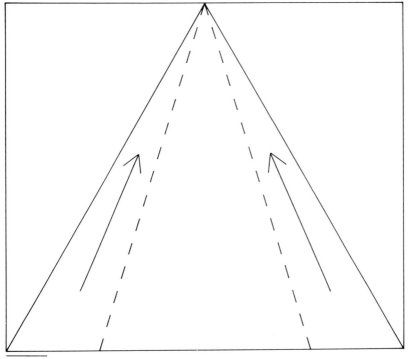

7. Kepes, p. 20.

This option restricts movement, however, inasmuch as each element of the composition relates to the perspective point. The background seems cramped, and all movement patterns tend toward the center of the stage, making it difficult to devise a free flow. This practice was common in the nineteenth century, but it sharply reduces the artistic choices available to the director.

If we rotate the space cube 45°, we immediately present the eye with a limitless view.

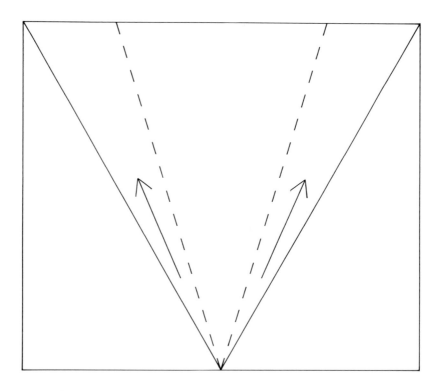

Here the compelling lines of direction expand. The eye enters the cube at its nearest apex where the closest forms are located, and continues outward for infinity. Lest the eye wander from his control, however, the careful artist will bend its gaze back into the space cube, leading it from one object to another in a classic whirling spiral.

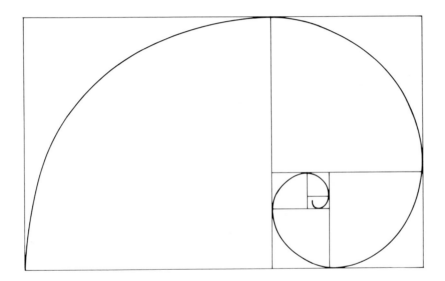

Thus, with his frame as referent, the director establishes a dominant contour. As the eye enters the frame, the director leads it along a line that moves from principal object to principal object, taking care that the entire image is scanned, but in the order and with the relationships he intended. The perception is most satisfying when the eye is led from the frontal plane to the background by a suggested line of gaze, without the need for the eye to do more than wander over the image. The dominant contour ties subunits of the composition together, thus unifying the entire visual field, at the same time permitting the eye to explore secondary units of interest without inhibiting the perception of the whole.

For developing sensitivity to a dominant contour, the Japanese practice of cutting small units of composition from larger arrangements is helpful. It encourages the student to discover not only those small compositions but how they make up the large image. By contrast, those who lack skill in composition will create images having no relationships; if asked to illustrate a poem they will set down a series of complete and isolated units representing images suggested by the poem, but these will not document the total image of the poem which the poem's own images generate.

The edge of the dominant contour is seen as *line,* and the direction of a line can be highly expressive of the quality the artist wants perceived.

This vertical line suggests dignity, grandeur, a balance of forces that might break into action at any time.

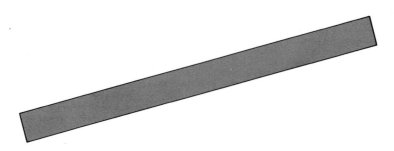

This diagonal line is action. Most people, when asked, state that this line if going "uphill," although why it is perceived that way is unknown. Perhaps our habit of reading from left to right conditions that response.

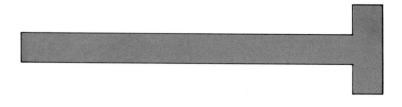

Similarly, when asked which side represents the "end" of this line, most people point to the right.

This horizontal line has acted. It conveys a restful, tranquil, stable quality.

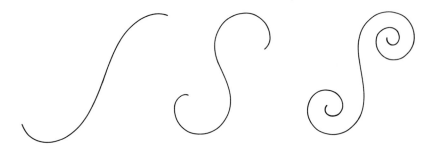

Curved lines are feminine. They can evoke a staccato quality of unrest.

Or they can suggest the dignity of flowing movement.

It is useful, then, to know the response lines evoke. Draw a line. Observe its quality and personality and what it reveals about you. Look at the edges of things, hurriedly, not to see their every element but to discover the squareness of a table, the cylinders of a lamp, how light defines the roundness of an apple.

In their simplest forms lines can be classified as follows:

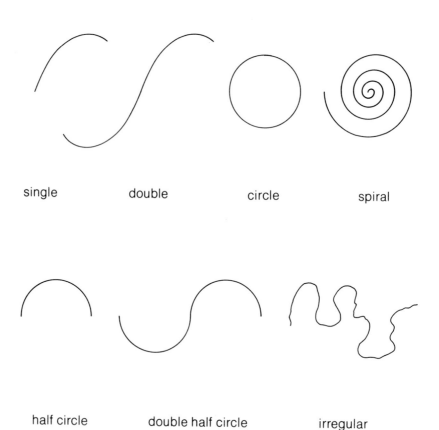

single   double   circle   spiral

half circle   double half circle   irregular

116

On stage, of course, line structure is complex. The setting, the proscenium, the stage floor, the actors' bodies, their movement patterns, all contribute to the line sum. When choosing a line or line pattern to convey or reinforce the dominant quality of the scene, the *average* of line bias is the key. A pyramid, although it has some diagonal lines, is essentially vertical. That fact helps explain its solid grandeur.

Within the dominant contour and by means of expressive line, the spectator's eye is led to the point of greatest interest. On stage this point usually is the speaking character, and line is the chief means of directing attention to him. In a scene showing four men studying a set of plans, their degree of concentration will appear in the general line their bodies make as they bend together over the table. The more intense their scrutiny, the more apparent the line. As they conclude and relax, the line they established will wander. Thus line, an objective correlative of their feelings, directs our attention to the point of greatest interest.

But line is only one of several resources for establishing emphasis, and emphasis is important because if an element of the composition is not noticed almost immediately, it is likely not to be noticed at all. The stage picture, constantly changing, is a veritable field of competition for the spectator's eye.

The more intense the stimulus, the better chance it has of being seen. This point is hardly revolutionary, but it is important. An intense color, an unusual form, a moving object will always take attention away from those having fewer such qualities. The larger the object, the better chance it has of being seen.

The longer the duration of a stimulus, the better chance it has of commanding attention. The more frequently a stimulus appears — especially if it is an interesting stimulus — the better chance it has of being perceived.

Directors commonly place two characters in dialogue so that they seem to share the scene equally. In my view, this practice is usually unwise. Two points of equal importance merely divide audience interest. Prominence should be given one figure. The point of emphasis can be quickly shifted from one character to another by means of movement, position, expression, light, or elevation; but one figure should always have emphasis.

This goal is made easier by the fact that the eye tends to move toward the axis of a curve, or to the apex of a rectangle. Thus a figure commands additional interest when it is placed at a point where lines converge.

However emphasis is achieved, space must be organized to be satisfying, that is, all elements of the composition are brought into proper balance. This does not mean that an artistic director will never present an unbalanced scene; it does mean that he will never ignore what the degree of balance or imbalance he presents means to his audience.

Balance does have meaning. It carries profound psychological weight. During World War II, Axis soldiers, knowing that others could not resist straightening crooked pictures, attached booby traps to them that detonated the charge. Why we strive for manifest balance is conjectural. Perhaps the semicircular canals of the inner ear are so sensitive to imbalance, however perceived, that they induce a fear of falling even when no actual danger is present.

Thus, darker objects seem heavier than lighter objects, and, therefore, this picture seems to be too heavy to the right:

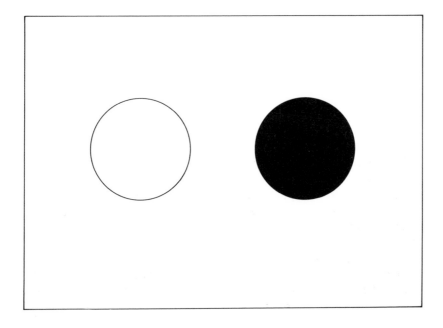

This drawing gives no relief to the eye (and reinforces the earlier observation that any composition requires a definite point of emphasis):

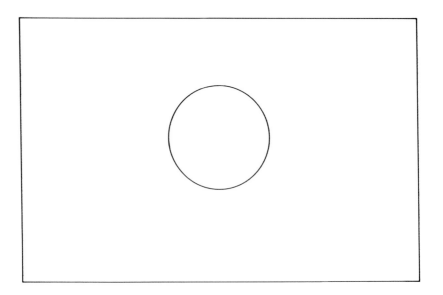

The principle is worth stressing. The balance easiest to achieve is an equal distribution of weight on both sides of the field of vision. But equal division of space is not composition. The field is, in fact, not composed at all; it is merely divided. When we balance every value, one cancels out the other, and the arrangement becomes inert and unexpressive.

Painters theorize that the left side of a painting seems heavier than the right side. They describe this portion of the field of vision as the *Golden Section* — an area 38% from the left and 62% from the right. Here the eye enters the space cube easily and comes comfortably to rest because, it is said, the proportions of the golden section parallel the proportions of man's own body. By his measurements are defined the cubit (from the elbow to the tip of the middle finger), the foot, and the span (from the tip of the thumb to the tip of the little finger).

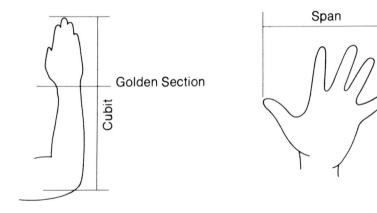

Golden Section

Cubit

Span

In a definition of the golden section, the span is to the foot as the foot is to the cubit.

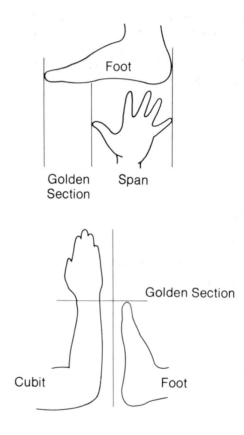

Golden
Section   Span

Golden Section

Cubit   Foot

   Because of its harmony with natural proportions, the golden
section is an effective place for a center of attention. Balance is
achieved by structuring a lighter weight and generous space to the
right (stage left) of it. The practice is consistent with Saxe
Meiningen's admonition that an actor should never be placed
directly down center, and is easily discerned in the paintings of
Rembrandt, Van Dyke, Monet, and other masters.

122

It is also consistent with the convention of composing according to the *Rule of Thirds.* If we intersect the field of vision with lines beginning one-third of the distance from every border, we establish dominant contours along which the main compositional elements should lie.

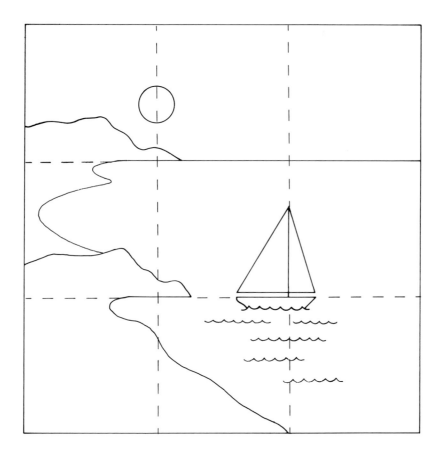

The technique is simple and effective. It provides balance, a dominant contour, and an expressive line. The field of view expands, the eye is encouraged to move in a whirling spiral; yet the composition seems easy and unpremeditated. It does not assure emphasis, but it adds still another to the director's options for structuring emphasis, and it generates an interesting, psychologically complex image.

Conventional stage space, because three-dimensional and usually rectangular, offers additional communicative means. The right angles formed by the corners of the stage are natural arrows. Thus any form or line, as it approaches a corner, becomes increasingly significant because of the dynamism it receives from the other forces converging there.

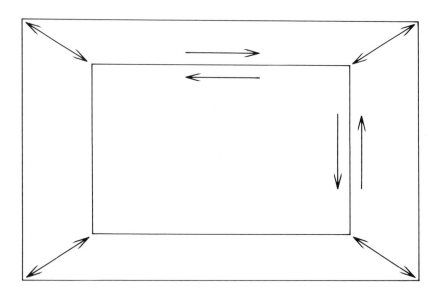

The four corners of the stage floor architecturally support four vertical lines, and a figure placed in relationship to any of these values immediately acquires a new quality. For example, the two verticals symmetrically frame an actor entering from upstage center. Should he stand in either upstage corner his entire being is made more important, for he is energized by the strong verticals. He appears to draw both physical and spiritual strength from them.

The two upper corners, far more than the downstage two, convey a strong impression of significant beginnings because they have not only two verticals but lines racing to them from various parts of the stage to form right angles — always makers of conflict and power. There are two of these from the top and two at the stage level, which, with the two verticals, make six strong supports in the upper

two corners. Add to these one more factor: the invisible diagonals which stream from the upper corners to the lower. . . . Note some changes in emphasis as this figure walks slowly on its diagonal way. Two steps away from the corner the six supporting lines no longer operate, and the figure is alone. . . .[8]

This is not to say that the character is weakened; as he steps out, the laws which make the central area powerful take over. Furthermore, if he moves with a slight twisting motion, he measurably heightens the spectators' ability to perceive his plasticity.[9] But I cannot agree with Humphrey that exact center stage, even down front, confers most potency upon him. She writes:

Have a figure walk slowly down center from back to front. When farthest away he is mysterious, with a high dynamic and symbolic potential, much more so than if he were off center. As he advances, the electrically charged center takes over and he increases in stature and power. As he advances to the apron, all this vanishes and the personal takes over.[10]

My experience, however, is that a figure dead center, where all forces converge, is static, trite, and two-dimensional. Indeed, he is anti-expressive. As we have noted throughout this chapter, all seeing — all composition — derives from space-object relationships. A figure in equal contact with every force has a special relationship to none.

These principles of space organization are universal and apply, of course, to any composition placed on stage. But they are especially

---

8. Doris Humphrey, *The Art of Making Dances* (New York: Holt, Rinehart and Winston, 1959), pp. 74–76.

9. Hans Wallach and D. N. O'Connell, "The Kinetic Depth Effect," *Journal of Experimental Psychology* 45 (1953):205–17.

10. Humphrey, p. 80.

127

relevant, in the context of this work, to the design of space so as to arrange before us abstract theatrical works.

By manipulating space properly we can suggest dynamism, imply gender, determine the emphasis and balance compositional elements will have, generate movement among static objects, and force the field of vision to expand or contract. And, by creating inversely from each of these qualities, we find substance in the meaning of space itself — such as the comfortable proportions of the golden section, the irresistible power of the whirling spiral, or the emotional impact of the diagonal line — for new artistic statements that can be embellished and amplified by other constructs of theatre.

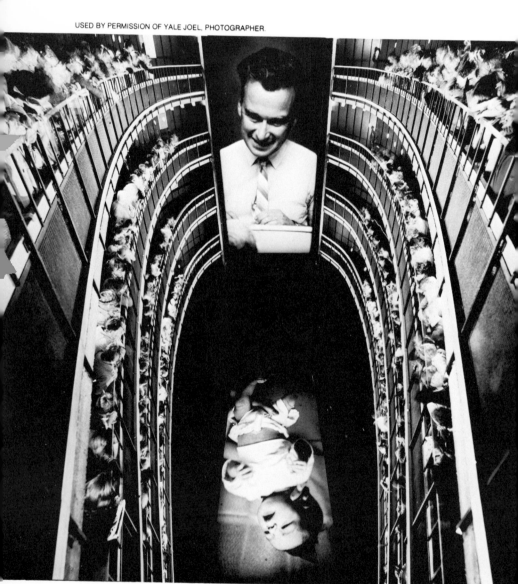

Innovative space relationship.

8
STAGE-AUDITORIUM-
AUDIENCE
RELATIONSHIPS

One national television show has a sure-fire technique for developing audience homogeneity. Shortly before the program is videotaped, the show's director asks everyone in the audience to turn around and shake hands with the person in the row behind him. That is, of course, impossible to do. But the attempt creates an awkward predicament in which one laughs at oneself and others.

A similar tactic for molding people into a group is to ask each person to extend his hand and then shake hands with the one to his right. The typical person is embarrassed because he cannot, and often he laughs at his gullibility, then shakes hands with those on both sides of him.

The problem of audience relationships and perception is substantial and significant. Our objective, we said, is to bring the audience to a predetermined response. One large step toward that goal is to insure that the audience perceives the production in a reasonably predictable way. It is, for example, possible to influence audience objectivity by varying its seating pattern, or by manipulating the density of the spectator-group. Without a companion, we know, one is less likely to express an overt response to a filmed comedy at a drive-in movie.

Harry Levi Hollingworth says, "Social sympathy is promoted by physical closeness which, therefore, favors the emotional appeal; logical persuasion is better encouraged by separating the members of the audience more widely." Furthermore, "Elevation of the performer above the floor level favors his prestige and often gives influence to his suggestions; dispensing with the platform, on the other hand, favors that mode of *rapport* in which the audience takes strong initiative."[1]

Tyrone Guthrie wrote:

Plush tip-ups with arms take up valuable space; besides they induce languor. An audience feels excitement in proportion as it is

---

1. Harry Levi Hollingworth, *The Psychology of the Audience* (Chicago: American Book Company, 1935), p. 170–72.

crowded; broadly speaking, the tighter it is squeezed, the more receptive it is to the infection of mass-excitement. There must be an optimum point at which excitement is highest before physical discomfort becomes so intense as to distract attention. This optimum point should be the aim of a theatre architect.[2]

The truth of this assertion is nowhere more apparent than at a football game when one compares the behavior of the crowd packed into the bleachers with that of the crowd occupying spacious chair seats. It's possible, of course, that because chair seats are expensive, the differences are due to age and a sense of decorum. But because many faculty and townspeople now sit with the students, it appears that age and manners alone cannot account for the restraint of the chair section and the ebullience of the bleacher section.

There are moments of record when people in groups no longer perceive as individuals. This phenomenon has artistic potential. Some factors that generate this audience-condition are 1) the size or intensity of the stimulus, 2) the degree of social anonymity the character and the behavior of the group permit, 3) the regimentation imposed upon the group ("A group forced into similar actions tends to respond more easily to a given stimulus"), and 4) the degree to which the group is susceptible to emotional contagion. When several of these factors meet they bring about an *audience-condition* with the result that people in groups are more uncritically receptive to stimuli than when alone. They react to visual and auditory spectacle more enthusiastically than when alone. They are more commonplace in their sentiment and their opinions. They are more partisan than when alone, and they tend to take sides for or against what they perceive.

All other factors being equal, groups are especially open to suggestion and therefore easily led. This principle was discovered

2. Tyrone Guthrie, "Shakespearean Production," in *The Year's Work In The Theatre: 1949–50* (London: Longmans, Green, 1950), p. 40.

and exploited by Adolf Hitler, and I am personally dismayed that audience response has been more systematically studied by political demagogues than by artists hoping to communicate. Thus a group audience-condition affects perception, and actor-audience proximity affects the condition.

The practice of placing the audience at one end of an auditorium while viewing the action at another seems to be the logical culmination of the "ideal viewing place" concept generated by the one-point perspective of the Renaissance. Fortunately recent trends in theatre architecture are leading us away from that tradition. The arena configuration, the peripheral (as advocated by Artaud), the thrust, and the open stage all encourage an implied if not a genuinely close proximity between actors and audience. The empty-room concept advocated by the Russian director, Nikolai Okhlopkov, seems to be the ultimate approach to flexibility and to an audience-stage relationship determined by the requirements of each play.

Fortunately, too, some of the virtues of vertical and overhead movement are explored by Walter Gropius in his design for a total theatre,[3] and, to a lesser degree, in the National Theatre at Chichester, England. Some recent open-stage theatres in America permit overhead action.

Moholy-Nagy prophesied: "The next form of the advancing theatre — in cooperation with future authors — will probably answer the above demands with suspended bridges and drawbridges running horizontally, diagonally, and vertically within the space of the theatre; with platform stages built far into the auditorium; and so on."[4]

Such concepts are not entirely new. As early as 1663 Joseph Furttenbach envisioned an octagonal recreation hall equipped with four stages and a turntable in the center of which spectators sat and feasted while viewing the production. And he described auditoriums

---

3. Walter Gropius, ed., *The Theatre of the Bauhaus* (Middletown, Conn.: Wesleyan University Press, 1961), p. 13.

4. Ibid., p. 68.

having holes in the ceiling through which perfumed water was sprayed on the spectators — an involvement tactic surprisingly contemporary.[5]

So attempts have been made to discover the means by which an audience can be brought to a predetermined effect, and the impact audience-stage relationships have upon that effect. Gropius wrote: "An audience will shake off its inertia when it experiences the surprise effect of space transformed. By shifting the scene of action during the performance from one stage position to another and by using a system of spotlights and film projectors, transforming walls and ceiling into moving picture scenes, the whole house would be animated. . . . Thus the playhouse itself, made to dissolve into the shifting illusionary space of the imagination, would become the scene of action itself."[6]

And attempts have been made to implement others of the principles I have mentioned. In an experimental production, the audience entered an arena theatre which had been converted for this production into a multipurpose room. It contained no seats; the audience sat on the floor or on pillows. The audience was packed as closely together as possible. Resistance to this request was slight, and the closer people sat, the more enthusiastically they responded. The production lasted only an hour and twenty minutes so as not to tax the audience, but this seating arrangement — plus other devices such as dancing in which the audience participated, the passing of objects from one to another, the touching of hands, and participation in rhythmic exercises — generated a homogeneity that contributed significantly to the production's favorable reception.

The values communicated by touching are seldom considered in the theatre, even though psychotherapy teaches that touch is fundamental to communication. It is now fashionable to communicate through touch the social concern we should have for

5. A. M. Nagler, "The Furttenback Theatre in Ulm," *The Theatre Annual* II (1953):46–47.

6. Gropius, p. 12.

each other. One way to express this concern is to place an emotionally disturbed person among a group of people who are holding hands, and then to ask him to break loose by running against the ring. Because he cannot, because he is literally imprisoned by the arms of his fellows, he learns of his dependency upon others and of their concern for him.

Or, when caring for an emotionally disturbed child, attendants sometimes seize him when he misbehaves or tries to harm himself by thrusting his head or body against a wall or object, pinning his arms to his sides, and holding him in a loving embrace until he realizes the futility and hostility of his acts. This practice is proving to be more effective in reducing emotional disturbance than are straightjackets, restraining sheets, or padded cells. One difference, of course, is that the child is touched by human beings, thus promoting a kind of communication that no other process generates.

Some of the most promising investigation of audience-stage relationships is being done in multi or mixed media. Abel Gance used a split movie screen as early as the 1920s in Paris, but multi images are now used so imaginatively that the most artistic aspect of the 1967 World's Fair in Canada was the imaginative use of fragmented imagery. The most effective were not always the most technically complex. Nevertheless, the multiple screen technique expands current anarchic techniques of staging which challenge the viewer to make what he will from the multiaction which surrounds him.

The technique of electronic multiple imagery enables the expression of an artist's perception of *what is*, which invites a viewer's conclusion about *what means*. This is a theme that I have tried to amplify throughout this work. Artistic images need not always create a story; they need not produce an illusion. They can be constructs for an imaginative synthesis and interpretation by the perceptor. As Alain Robbe-Grillet observed: ''(Now the world is neither meaningful nor absurd), it simply is. . . . In place of this universe of meanings (psychological, social, functional), one should try to construct a more solid, more immediate world. So that first of

Inside this projection house reclining spectators view projections on the ceiling of the dome

136

all it will be through their presence that objects and gestures will impose themselves. . . ."[7] Or, as attributed to the paintings of Jackson Pollock, "By-passing the anxiety of turning thought and feeling into signs and symbols, Pollock started to weave vast nets in which all image possibilities would be mapped and trapped."[8]

At Expo-67 images were displayed without discursive intent. Stories were told in illogical sequences and viewers were thrown off balance mentally — sometimes physically. Evidently pictures in such sequences remain in mind well after the performance is over, although it may take some time for the viewer to sort them out and decide what meaning he will attribute to them. Sometimes their meaning cannot be verbalized. The images are only what they are — images. One twenty-minute film set sight against sight, image against image, in a successful attempt to suggest but not explicate the turbulent sensibilities of the young without using conventional narrative.

The Czech Pavilion's Kino-automat there permitted each viewer to be his own director. The movie consisted of five incidents. At the end of each the film stopped, and the audience voted on how it should continue. The hero asked the audience if he were to blame for the plot's mishaps, and the audience decided whether he should go free. Thus, the technique required the audience to make moral judgments and to decide fate.

The cinematic close-up is another manipulation of proximity worthy of the theatre's emulation. We present equivalents of close-ups when we bring actors downstage or light them with emphatic color or intensity, but surely the theatre should also provide a moveable area platform, or tray, that enables the director to swing important scenes into the literal midst of the audience. A device somewhat like these was used effectively in the Lincoln Center production of *Danton's Death.* There important scenes were mechanically thrust sharply forward to the front of the stage so that

---

7. "It's What's There," *Life,* 28 July 1967, p. 44A.
8. "Flight to Freedom," *Newsweek,* 20 January 1964, p. 81.

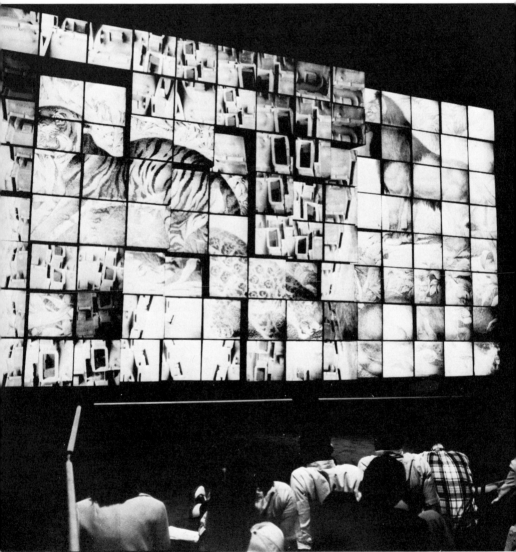

Motorized ever-changing projected mosaic.

Projected closeup. Patricia Oatman, actress. James Hayes, photographer.

Participatory theatre, Brigham Young University.

the audience acquired a compelling perception of the action.

Furthermore, better use can be made of movies or of television during moments of climactic emotional intensity, such as Romeo's and Juliet's first kiss. An enlarged cinematic or televised image of their kiss would enable a fuller perception of their experience, while, at the same time, their smaller, more distant, bodies remain apparent to the audience.

Prophetic, perhaps, of that art that attempts not to narrate but to provide raw material from which the perceptor makes his own art experience is the Fun Palace envisioned by Joan Littlewood. She foresees a building that will enable the audience to design its own experience. It will have, for example, a science area full of games and tests that challenge the industry and war forces in man; a music area, a learning area, an acting area, and a plastic area in which the childhood joys of touching, handling, and making from paint, clay, stone, and textiles can be reconstructed. Within this structure nothing shall last more than ten years. Everything will be intended to be manipulated and consumed. An important part of the palace will be closed-circuit television showing coal miners, woodmen, and doctors actually at work, and the comings and goings outside various clubs and hospitals. Finally there will be zones of quiet for those who don't feel like listening to music or taking part actively.[9]

---

9. Joan Littlewood, " 'Theatre' or Fun Palace?" *Play Bill* 2 (April 1965) 4:49.

Visual rhythms.

9
RHYTHM

Rhythm in the theatre is so general a term that its imprecise definition suggests imprecise use of it as an artistic medium. It is used often to characterize any regularly recurring stimulus, whether it be language, movement, or scenic element. This application is incorrect, however, and regrettable, for no principle is more useful to the creative director who would bring his audience to a reasonably predictable response. A regularly recurring pattern is the antithesis of rhythm, for rhythm, by definition, constitutes an interruption or modification of a recurring pattern.

The Greek word *rhythmos* means "measured motion," although classical theorists generally understood rhythm to be a *bond*, meaning a restraint or interruption imposed on an established stimulus, whether of sound, vision, or other sensation. The steady drone of a tuning fork is not rhythmical, for it is uninterrupted sound, and the chaos of an earthquake is merely unorganized noise. Thus rhythm is characterized by an orderly recurrence of stimuli which is periodically interrupted or restrained by a departure from sequence.

Such artful interruptions can influence an audience strongly, for once a sensory stimulus is established, man yearns to perpetuate it. Within its order he finds comfort. When the basic stimulus pattern is inhibited or altered by the bond of rhythm, his well-being is threatened and he longs for the reestablishment of order. When the bond, restraint, or inhibition is lifted from the pattern, the former sense of pleasure returns, this time more precious than before. The experience is one of contraction followed by relaxation; it is a pattern of effort, fruition, then rest.[1]

Recall Doris Humphrey's statement that, as a dancer, ". . . my entire technique consists of the development of the process of

---

1. "Tempo" and "rhythm" are sometimes used, incorrectly, as synonyms. Rhythm is a pattern imposed on stimuli, a recurrent alternation of thesis and arsis, or, in art, a "regular recurrence of like features in a composition." Tempo means literally, "time," pace, or *rate* of movement. A 3/4 or waltz rhythm may be delivered at a fast or slow tempo without altering its rhythmic structure.

falling away from and returning to equilibrium."[2] This fall from equilibrium is an "exciting danger," the recovery from which is "repose and peace." In music, too, melodies are composed by departing from the basic or original chord, thus creating such a strong desire to return to the original that only adventuresome composers will deny that satisfaction. When we count waltz time, beats two and three make up the recurring pattern or stimulus which is inhibited periodically by count one.

We respond to these tensions and resolutions in many ways, most of them restrained and unrecognized. We breathe with the rhythm, sometimes we keep time with our tongue, or by tapping our toe. In one way or another we are compelled to respond to any clearly rhythmical stimulus with physical — that is, muscular — action.

That artist, then, who commands a participating, not a passive, audience, may manipulate its muscular participation by selecting and controlling the art work's rhythm. Dance and popular musicians make this a pleasant and satisfying process; their music is popular precisely because of a heavily accented rhythm. Even those who disdain contemporary music succumb — to the extent of a tapping toe — to simple rhythm's lure.

In addition, rhythm induces certain feeling-states — probably because feelings cannot be separated from their physical expression. The exact nature of rhythmically induced emotion is somewhat controversial. Stanislavski believed that "tempo-rhythm excites not only your emotion memory . . . but it also brings your visual memory and its images to life."[3] If this theory is true, then appropriate rhythms may be used repeatedly to liberate previously known feelings. Henry Lanz, however, declares that rhythm does not

---

2. Doris Humphrey, "My Approach to the Modern Dance," in *Dance: A Basic Educational Technique,* ed. Frederick Rand Rogers (New York: Macmillan Co., 1941), p. 189.

3. Constantin Stanislavski, *Building a Character,* trans. Elizabeth Reynolds Hapgood (New York: Theatre Arts Books, 1949). The references to Stanislavski in this chapter are based on his two chapters on rhythm in this work, pp. 177–237.

reconstruct past emotions, but creates new feeling-states which have no existence apart from the rhythm itself.[4] Whatever the history or source of the emotion, there is abundant evidence that, through exposure to strong rhythmic stimuli, one can be led through significant emotional experiences.

Incidentally, Carl Seashore, who conducted many studies into its psychology, adds that rhythm favors perception by grouping; it periodically adjusts the strain of attention; it gives us a feeling of balance and grace; it gives us a feeling of freedom, luxury, and power. It excites and makes us insensible to the excitation. (It makes us want to dance, for example, and gives us the power to dance without becoming tired.) It makes the commonplace interesting, and it makes play out of work. (It may motivate one to rehearse, because the act of rehearsing becomes pleasant and satisfying.)[5]

Rhythm is a helpful index of emotion because the spontaneous rhythms of the body are reflections of mental and emotional states, generating, as one's mind or feelings change, a synchronous change in one's physical manifestation of rhythm. Of course these relationships are not constant, predictable, or easily classified. But to most people odd and irregular patterns of rhythm suggest the presence of complex, intense emotion. We find a count of five or seven beats per measure more stimulating than two or four. An odd number of beats to a measure generates excitement, suspense, and anticipation; and when the final beats in a measure are emphasized, the emotions of excitement, suspense, and anticipation are given additional impetus. If, however, we want to develop feelings of grandeur, solidarity, and well-being, we exploit even-metered measures and generally accent the first beat.

How then, does the artist choose and manifest appropriate

-----

4. Henry Lanz, *The Physical Basis of Rime* (London: Oxford University Press, 1931), p. 298.
5. Carl Seashore, *Psychology of Music* (New York: McGraw-Hill, 1938), pp. 140–45. This list is a condensation of the original.

rhythms? "The rhythm is the person," says the poetess Marianne Moore. It is the director's personal concept of the script that determines what rhythms are appropriate. He considers the rise and fall of tension and plot progression in the play's structure, of course, and he tries to count or at least sense the rhythms inherent in characterizations, and in the intellectual, emotional, and mood values of the drama.[6]

He studies the rhythmic patterns of his settings, his costumes, his colors, and especially the cadence of the dialogue. In verse drama the rhythm is formally defined. In prose the director requires much sensitivity to discover the rhythmic patterns of the speech, probably reading the lines aloud frequently until he crystallizes his conclusions.

According to interpretation he emphasizes the rhythm of the play's locale, or he may derive movement and business from the personal rhythms of his actors, for the gifted actor usually will introduce correct rhythms subconsciously for his performance of a character, and the director need not suggest any change.

So much confidence did Rouben Mamoulian, producer of *Porgy and Bess* and *Oklahoma!*, have in actors' rhythms, as manifest in speech, movement, or feeling, that he ordered effects or mood music composed for the play by one who had attended rehearsals and determined the prevailing rhythmic patterns.[7] This same philosophy guides the movie industry, where scenes are photographed "on location" to incorporate moods and rhythms too subtle to be reproduced in studios, and where accompanying music is composed afterward to complement what the camera records.

––––––––

6. Alexander Dean, *Fundamentals of Play Directing* (New York: Farrar and Rinehart, 1941), pp. 284–96, and Ruth Klein, *The Art and Technique of Play Directing* (New York: Rinehart, 1953), pp. 101–10, offer help in making these analyses. Rhythmic problems encountered when reciting iambic pentameter are carefully analyzed in Wallace A. Gray, "Concepts of Rhythm: The Past Fifty Years," in *Re-Establishing The Speech Profession*, Robert T. Oliver and Marvin G. Bauer, eds. (New York: Speech Association of the Eastern States, 1959), pp. 87–89.

7. Rouben Mamoulian, "Rhythm, Music, and the Theatre," *Etude*, 63 (April, 1945):187.

Guided by these impressions, the director requires his actors to create identical rhythms or contrasting rhythms, or he may change the rhythms from scene to scene. He need not formally explain in terms of beats per measure the rhythm he conceives, but he must assure that through his or his actors' creativity appropriate rhythms are manifest. The only grievous and common error is to take no account of rhythm, letting it occur by chance, for this malfeasance permits unexciting, undisciplined performances.

The logical beginning place is in the training we give our actors, where, through practice with rhythm, we help them achieve physical and emotional flexibility. I have already described the possibility of arousing powerful emotions through the use of rhythm. This practice was evidently a standard part of Stanislavski's instruction: two chapters of his *Building A Character* are devoted to descriptions of exercises wherein the students make with their hands the rhythms of places they have visited and experiences they have had. He points out that a declaration of war, a solemn gathering, the reception of a deputation, each has its distinctive rhythm. Musicians' training in rhythm, Stanislavski writes, is one reason why opera casts are able to perform with fewer rehearsals than are actors.

There are, of course, standard techniques for teaching rhythm by means of percussion and movement exercises, and a scene where actors are to interrupt one another will profit if the actors walk the rhythm of their speeches in counterpoint so that they set the opposition of the rhythms into their nerves and muscles. An actress will intensify a scene's growing tension by doubling once and even twice the number of steps she takes without increasing the length or timing of the movement.

However, Eugene Vakhtangov, the Russian director, was much opposed to developing rhythm through "beautiful" movements. In his studio, "students would move furniture in a certain rhythm accompanied by music, would clean the room, serve the table and so on. Vakhtangov would try to see that it was done with the freedom, lightness, and spontaneity with which such movements are executed in life." . . . Rhythmicality is the property of each and

Space-rhythm rehearsal. *W-2 Form.* Brigham Young University. Lael J. Woodbury, director.

every movement in nature. It is necessary to learn to live in a given rhythm and not only to move in it. To eat, to drink, to work, to gaze, to hear, to think — in other words — to live rhythmically."[8]

Suggestions given thus far are for the director's use when he is training and rehearsing the actor. Other uses for rhythm occur during production. Mamoulian's production of *Porgy and Bess,* for example, made bold use of rhythm to bring the audience into harmony with the action of the play:

Catfish Row . . . is part of the story. The gradually increasing rhythm of its awakening, with the beat caught up from the orchestra in the shuffle of a broom, the rasp of a saw, the smack of a polishing cloth on a shoe tip, the slap of a paddle on a carpet, the final beat of clogging feet — this is part of the story too. The empty rocking chairs which, fancifully grotesque, catch up the rhythm of one of the songs and beat time of their own accord; the prayers of the crap shooters to the bones; the cries and shuffles of the men and women selling crabs and strawberries — all these are at once background and story, and, in a fashion, music, too.[9]

Rhythm is especially valuable for suggesting that all actors in a scene live in the same world, and this quality is enhanced if the director is meticulous about rhythm patterns during entrances and transitions. Too often the actor brings with his entrance the rhythms of the dressing room, or of an offstage conversation. Makeup and dressing-room chatter and backstage horseplay, the rhythm-conscious director discovers, are incompatible with stable, delicately constructed and artistic work. Several famous Russian actors — Shchepkin, Sadovski, Shumski — were careful to arrive in the wings

---

8. Eugene Vakhtangov, "Preparing for the Role," in *Acting: A Handbook of the Stanislavski Method,* ed. Toby Cole (New York: Lear Publishers, 1947), pp. 121–22.

9. Richard Lockridge, quoted in Barnard Hewitt, *Theatre U.S.A.* (New York: McGraw-Hill, 1959), p. 398.

well ahead of their entrances so that they could catch the rhythm of the performance before entering.

Indeed, Stanislavski advises actors to assemble before performances and during intermissions to do exercises with music calculated to develop in them correct tempi-rhythms. These, he suggests, should be something in the nature of sitting-up exercises. And when the actor is on the stage, he should, if speaking after a long pause, accent the rhythm of his speech so that both he and the audience will remain aware that the pattern is being sustained.

Rhythms of movement and grouping require as much artistry as the rhythms of speech. Jaques-Dalcroze, who believed that a gesture completed out of rhythm produces a positive "aesthetic pain," was openly hostile to those who study rhythm only to become graceful. He saw rhythm on the stage as a means of communication, especially in group scenes, and advised that "generally speaking, dynamic effects are obtained by modifications of space, and emotive effects by interruptions of continuous symmetrical formations."[10]

The emotional impact of interrupted symmetry is intensified on the stage by countermovement and contrasting gestures. "An advancing body will convey a far stronger impression of its forward direction if simultaneously other bodies are seen retiring," wrote Dalcroze. "A single person rising gently out of the kneeling group will produce a stronger impression than if the whole rose at the same moment. The effect will be increased tenfold, if while he rises, those who remain kneeling bow themselves to the ground."

Dalcroze credits Adolphe Appia with pioneering the use of rhythms in crowds, and says that he used the chorus to set the mood for Wagner's music-dramas. By the use of polyrhythm, or rhythmic counterpoint between the gestures of the individual and the crowd, he was able to communicate new and subtle emotional values.

If the director wishes, he may clarify and emphasize mood and

----

10. Jacques-Dalcroze, quoted in *Rhythm, Music and Education*, trans. Harold F. Rubenstein (New York: G. P. Putnam's Sons, 1921), pp. 225–26.

action by the rhythm of the stage setting itself, according to Alexander Tairov, founder of the Moscow Kamerny Theatre:

If the spectator is to receive the impression that she (the Madonna) is drifting down, scarcely touching the ground with her feet; if the descendant is to have a solemnly liturgical quality, the steps and platforms must be so constructed that their dimensions will have a constant relationship throughout; their rhythmic relationship should be expressed in terms of 1 to 4 or 1 to 8, so that the movements of the actress may in turn acquire a regular and flowing rhythm. On the other hand let us imagine that we wish to impart to the stage the quality of a stormy, passionate Bacchanal in honor of Dionysus. We must then break up the stage level in such a manner that the steps and platforms are united by manifold and varied rhythms. By this means the Bacchie gestures and satyr-like leaps on the stage acquire a complex rhythmic extravagance which evokes from the spectator the proper impression of a Bacchic action.[11]

In my experience there are two especially valuable and practical uses of rhythm, the first of which is to promote homogeneity within a scene. Probably all of us develop scenes that will not flow. Time after time the actors bungle their movement, forget their lines, or perform so insincerely that the scene is bereft of intensity and excitement. Of course the actors must master their movement and lines, but frequently the extra stimulus needed is simply a powerful rhythmic pattern that will fuse the diverse elements of the scene into an ensemble.

For this purpose it may be helpful to play selected music during rehearsals. Some insist that the performance mood music be played during rehearsals. But profound results are available to the director who personally and boldly creates the proper rhythm pattern himself — whether by snapping fingers, clapping hands,

---

11. Mordecai Gorelik, *New Theatres for Old* (New York: Samuel French, 1952), p. 299.

speaking, or, with some, by rapping the forestage with a stick.

This suggestion may appall those who delight in subtle manipulation of the actor's creativity, but each director should experiment with bold rhythmic patterns, for they may become major weapons in his armory of creative techniques. When this technique is used artistically, it can generate an amazing degree of excitement, order, and control.

(Certainly Stanislavski, a paragon of "creating from within," does not disparage external and mechanical sources of stimuli. He suggests that an "electrical conductor" be placed in the prompter's box which will flash lights according to prerecorded indications in the margin of the prompt-book and thus control the actor's rhythm-tempo. He also maintains that good actors radiate strong personal rhythms with the contagious power of drawing less gifted actors along with them.)

The second greatest practical value of rhythm may lie in its power to communicate profound emotion. Many fine actors, apparently without conscious effort, introduce strongly rhythmic emphasis into deeply emotional scenes, and by doing so very much increase their abilities to awaken emotional — even physical — responses in their audiences. When Willy Loman utters his farewell lines to Biff, the stresses within his spirit and body are so powerful that he almost sings or chants these lines:

Now when you kick off, boy,
I want a seventy-yard boot.
And get right down the field under the ball,
And when you hit,
Hit low and hit hard,
Because it's important, boy.
There's all kinds of important people
In the stands,
And the first thing you know. . . .[12]

12. Arthur Miller, "Death of a Salesman," in *A Treasury of the Theatre*, John Gassner, ed. (New York: Simon & Schuster, 1963), p. 1,098.

How can an audience help responding to such an elegy of love and spiritual torment? Part of the genius of the playwright lies in the rhythmic pattern created here. On the stage, as in life, the more profound the emotion, the more powerful the manifestation of rhythm. This principle holds true for both lyric and dramatic feelings, and to apply this knowledge judiciously to conventional language-drama, as well as to artfully structured abstract theatrical constructs or stimuli, is a praiseworthy creative art.

Visual music.

10
SOUND

The creative director aims to control the sensory stimuli perceived by the spectator so that he is able to bring him to a predetermined emotional response. This aim differs radically from those who prize traditional theatre, such as Dame Sybil Thorndike, who said in an interview: "Well, we feel the theatre is getting to depend too much on the eye and we want to get back to the word — and we concentrate on that with no scenery. The art of the theatre is primarily speech; the stage is the actor. The theatre depends on speech as the opera depends on singing. [When G.B.S. engaged me to understudy Ellen O'Malley in *Candida* he] sat me by him at rehearsals and held me absorbed and fascinated by his asides: 'It's the word that matters, don't forget that'; he made me feel one could act one's head off but if the 'word' wasn't significant the rest was just 'flag-doodle.' "[1]

Regrettably, however, as we saw in previous chapters, language — because it has to be interpreted — introduces an impediment to understanding. Because all interpretations of abstractions are subjective, it is axiomatic that there will be as many versions of meaning as there are interpreters. His clear recognition of this communication lapse motivated Artaud to conceive a theatre of the senses, a theatre of concrete expression, and it inspired Ionesco's *The Bald Soprano* and similar plays.

Susanne Langer approached the problem by quoting Lord Russell's response to the question: "What can be expressed in words?"

It may well be that there are facts that do not lend themselves to this very simple schema; if so, they cannot be expressed in language. Our confidence in language is due to the fact that it . . . shares the structure of the physical world, and therefore can express that structure. But if there be a world which is not physical, or not in space-time, it may have a structure which we can never hope to

---

1. *Sunday Times Magazine Section* (London), 8 July 1962, p. 21.

express or to know. . . . Perhaps that is why we know so much about physics and so little of anything else.[2]

And then she makes this important point about the inadequacy of language to express all things and the effectiveness of sound in producing an emotion:

I do believe that in this physical, space-time world of our experience there are things which do not fit the grammatical scheme of expression. But they are not necessarily blind, inconceivable, mystical affairs; they are simple matters which require to be conceived through some symbolistic schema other than discursive language . . . Language is by no means our only articulate product. . . . There is, however, a kind of symbolism peculiarly adapted to the explication of unspeakable things, though it lacks the cardinal virtue of language, which is denotation. The most highly developed type of such purely connotational semantic is music. . . . A genuine symbol can most readily originate where some object, sound, or act is provided which has no practical meaning, yet tends to elicit an emotional response, and thus hold one's undivided attention.[3]

J. Donovan agrees with Langer's view. Sound so powerfully affects the listener because he cannot avoid hearing it and need not attribute meaning to it. "The passivity of the ear," he wrote, "allowed auditory impressions to force themselves into consciousness in season and out of season, when they were interesting to the dominant desires of the animal and when they were not. These impressions got further into consciousness, so to speak, before desire could examine their right of entrance, than was possible for impressions which could be annihilated by a wink or a turn of the head."[4]

---

2. Susanne K. Langer, *Philosophy In A New Key* (New York: New American Library, 1948), p. 82.
3. Langer, p. 83.
4. Quoted in Langer, p. 116.

Essentially, this research merely verifies the conclusions described by Richard Wagner:

A subject which is comprehended merely by the intelligence can also be expressed merely through the language of words; but the more it expands into an emotional concept, the more does it call for an expression which in its final and essential fullness can alone be obtained through the language of sounds. Hereby the essence of that which the Word-Tone-Poet has to express results quite by itself: it is the Purely Human, freed from all conventions.[5]

In effect, then, sound structured into language is especially valuable as an artistic medium because *it works directly upon the perceptor's nervous system*; it does not have to circulate through the brain for decoding into subjective meanings. A scream does not only mean; a scream is. A sign, a moan, a groan, a sustained sound from whatever source need be neither more nor less than its concrete self. But unquestionably it has impact upon the spectator, and when artfully structured it can bring him to predetermined responses.

This concept is not revolutionary. There have been, in fact, several attempts to explore the tonal — as distinguished from the conceptual — significance of speech. The Dadaists, for example, created poems and dramatic scenes using only vowel sounds. They generated unique sound experiences, and expressed rather well their view that men, their language, and their lives have little discernable meaning.

Even more artful, probably, is the work of today's concrete poets. Inspired by Mallarmé, Apollinaire, Pound, and Joyce, they create in language not meaning but experience. Language for them is not symbol but matter.

Another imaginative innovation was created by Harry Partch for his production of *King Oedipus* in 1952. There he composed a full

---

5. Quoted in Cole and Chinoy, eds., *Directing the Play* (Indianapolis: The Bobbs-Merrill Co., 1953), p. 41.

score — including exact tone inflection and rhythm — for a spoken drama and developed a new musical scale and an orchestra of new instruments to play his microscaled music. His objective was to convey *in sound* the full emotional range of the spoken text. "The music," Partch said, "is conceived as emotional saturation, that is the particular province of dramatic music to achieve."[6]

These experiments are useful because they explore new uses of this neglected medium. Much more has been done in cinema, where the director is truly creative, than in our playwright's theatre to test this important statement by Richard Wagner: "A subject which is comprehended merely by the intelligence can also be expressed merely through the language of words; but the more it expands into an emotional concept, the more does it call for expression which in its final and essential fullness can alone be obtained through the language of sounds."[7]

But sheer sound is immediately valuable not to replace speech but to supplement it. Perhaps the most useful generalization for the creative director is this: *music sounds the way we feel.* And the converse of that principle is equally valuable: *we tend to feel the way music sounds.* This principle explains the peculiar satisfaction we derive from opera, and why we accept conventions there that are not tolerable in drama. The tenor who utters a distained and incredibly high note moments before dying on stage surely taxes credibility. But probably in no other way can he so brilliantly convey the spiritual agony he feels. And because he can generate aesthetically a comparable feeling within us, we do not ponder the artificiality of his act.

I see a close similarity between the closing aria in grand opera and the observation of Jean Anouilh in *Antigone* that in tragedy one cannot expect the police to rescue the protagonist at the last

---

6. W. Leach, "Music For Words, Perhaps," *Theatre Arts* 37 (January 1953): 66–68.

7. Quoted by B. H. Clark in *European Theories of the Drama*, rev. ed. (New York: Crown Publishers, 1947), p. 346.

moment. All he can do is howl, so inevitable is his fate. Essentially, the tenor's final note is a musical and gloriously beautiful cry from the soul.

This principle, that we will feel the way music sounds, has a wide application. It was consciously implemented by Vladimir Ussachevsky when he created the sound score for Tad Danielewski's movie of Sartre's *No Exit*:

His electronically produced love songs sing a love song, simulate a rhumba and a waltz, and evoke the deadly hiss of escaping gas, and relentlessly attack the nervous system with cat-like screeches, siren-like wails, and agonized moans. Through the imaginative and skillful use of his resources, Ussachevsky illustrates how the manipulations of sound electronically cannot only underscore an emotion but implant it as well.[8]

And that is the point. Sound can implant emotion. Sheer sound can actually and measurably influence the electrical conductivity of the human body as manifested by increased fluctuations in the psycho-galvanic reflex.[9] Furthermore, it can: (1) act as a calmative in states of irritation or excitement; (2) act as a mild excitant in conditions of depression; (3) act as a dangerous irritant in morbid states of mind; (4) act as a stimulant to work of an uncongenial kind, to endurance, perseverance, strength, and energy in domestic life.[10] In fact, unpleasant sounds can so work upon the body that they produce measurable hormonal changes similar to those occasioned by mental or physical stress.[11] (Incidentally, music not understood seems to have the same intellectual value as silence.

---

8. "The Sound of Hell," *Newsweek*, 10 December 1962, p. 86.
9. Charles Diserens, *A Psychology of Music* (Cincinnati: The Authors for the College of Music, 1939), p. 274.
10. Diserens, p. 68.
11. "Sound can Produce Physiological Responses," *School, Science, and Mathematics*, 59 (November 1959): 659.

It probably is not perceived as music, only as noise, and eventually it is ignored as we ignore any background noise.)

Sound's profound ability to create or alter feeling states is further illustrated by this verbal description of a Navajo Indian tradition:

The Navajo birth is an interesting ceremony. About two weeks before the child is to born, the singer comes to the home to offer a chant to Whiteshower Woman, sister of the Changing Woman Earth. The mother to be repeats the litany after the singer. Then during the birth, if labor is hard, the singer will come again and bid the mother chant after him. It would be very bad for the mother to falter in her prayer, and strong must be her concentration to remember each syllable. As her mind moves off her labor, she commends herself to Whiteshower Woman and is transported beyond the field of pain.[12]

The ability of sound to alter feelings is further documented by the experience of folk singer Judy Collins who participated in some of the civil rights movements in 1964.

"I had seen enough," Judy, who is twenty-five, said, "to suffer from total fear. I knew I was going to be shot at or beaten. My hands as we rode trembled so much I made myself change the guitar strings to keep them occupied." She and the others began to sing softly. "Ain't gonna let nobody turn me round . . . marching up to Freedom Land." Judy says: "It was then that I found out just a little of what freedom music can really mean. The music was the only way to settle the terror — to direct it."[13]

The affect applies to the actors as well as to the audience. John Reich, of the Goodman Memorial Theatre, says that he believes it mandatory to play music during rehearsals. And Shelley Winters

---

12. Sharon Black, "Between Two Worlds," Brigham Young University Radio Network Production, presented May 16, 1968, Provo, Utah.

13. "Without These Songs . . .," *Newsweek*, 31 August 1964, p. 74.

reports that George Stevens used music and recordings of Hitler's voice to prepare the actors emotionally to perform in the movie version of *The Diary of Anne Frank.*

It is clear, then, that sound can bring an audience to a predetermined response because it generates, itself, the very response aimed for. But sound achieves that goal in more than one way. According to the theory of montage advanced by Pudovkin, Eisenstein, and their contemporaries, visual or aural images which make up a montage can be so juxtaposed that that fact — the juxtapositon of those specific elements and not of any others — will evoke in the perception and feelings of the spectator a complete concept of the art work's theme.

In this way, the use of montage, sound — in addition to generating emotion — can actually parallel the way we think. In fact it will make us think the way the artist dictates we will think. Therefore these directors chose shots, sequences, sounds, and rhythms for their sensory impact, not just for their casual, time, or idea relationships. They sought to arouse the audience's nervous reflexes into responsiveness. For they knew that sound applied directly to the nervous system will structure a sequence of physiological sensations that create rather than depend upon thought.

Eisenstein conceived of montage as an actual duplication of the processes of thought. He believed that by tightly controlling light, sound, rhythm, and juxtaposition he could reconstruct the "inner monologue" that takes place beneath the placid surface of a movie's characters.

For his *An American Tragedy,* as an attempt to reveal and contrast Clyde's inner thoughts with his outer actuality — the boat, the girl sitting beside him, his actions — he specified this list of sounds:

. . . Sounds. Formless. Or with sound-images: with objectively representational sounds. . . . Then suddenly, definite intellectually formulated words — as "intellectual" and dispassionate as pronounced words. With a black screen, a rushing imageless visuality.

Then in passionate disconnected speech. Nothing but nouns. Or nothing but verbs. Then interjections. With zigzags of endless shapes, whirling along with these in synchronization. Then racing visual images over complete silence. Then linked with polyphonic sounds. Then polyphonic images. Then both at once. . . .

As if presenting inside the characters the inner play, the conflict of doubts, the explosions of passion, the voice of reason . . . and, at the same time, contrasting with the almost complete absence of outer action: a feverish inner debate behind the stony mask of the face.[14]

In view of these principles — that music sounds the way we feel and that it makes us feel the way it sounds, that it can generate emotions as well as represent them, and that it can be structured to parallel the way we think — we find infinite use of sound as artistic substance.

Moholy Nagy envisioned a theatre giving limitless resources to the sound artist. He dreamed of speaking or singing arc lamps, loud speakers conveying a variety of qualities placed under the seats or the floor of the auditorium, and new amplifying systems that would raise the audience's "acoustic surprise-threshold" so much that their value would eclipse other technical theatrical media. His prophecy is being fulfilled.

We saw in chapter six how Max Reinhardt used sound to establish an atmosphere appropriate to his play, thus conditioning his audience to a festival effect. The sound of trumpets, the call to prayer, the procession all conspired to prepare spectators for his production of *The Miracle.* This idea is expanded by Francis Fergusson's explanation of Richard Wagner's attempts with music to create a mood of harmony and to suspend disbelief:

The lights go down, the orchestra begins; and the hypnotic will of the artist induces that "musical mood" in which all actual or

---

14. Sergei Eisenstein, *Film Form* (New York: Harcourt, Brace and Co., 1949), p. 105.

*intelligible distinctions vanish. The distinction between audience
and stage vanishes too, and performers and auditors alike live the
one life of the music. By means of the music, Wagner as it were
bypasses not only the shrewd discriminations of daily life, but all the
values of the common world. He manipulates directly the morose
Innerlichkeit of the faithless population. This is the process which
psychologists describe as the formation of a mob: all the individuals
identify themselves, in intense emotion, with the will and feeling of
the leader.*[15]

Meyerhold carried this idea even further. He believed that in *No
Plays* the wild fury of the music transports the public into a world of
hallucination, and to this degree achieves the predetermined
response which is the director's objective.

Having united the audience in mood, sound quickly conveys the
intended production style. Leopold Jessner's revolutionary
production of *The Weavers* employed naturalistic sound so artfully
that the effect must have been electrifying in the scene where the
weavers move through and begin to destroy the house. He specified
the stamping of feet, quiet sobs, a muttered expression of frightened
despair, outcries, pounding of fists, the noise of shattered window-
panes, nervous laughter, shouts and cries, moans, breathless
outbursts, pleading wails of terror, a quiet and controlled voice for
contrast, short phrases suggesting repressed emotion, and the
breaking of glass with fists. All of this took place with hardly a word
of dialogue and yet, according to reviews of the period, the effect
was believable, persuasive, and deeply moving.

Vsevlod Meyerhold also manipulated naturalistic sounds to
create a special mood, quality, or, if you will, world for his production
of *The Inspector General*. He specified, for example:

*When everybody says: "What, an inspector," there should be no
uniformity. There should be a variety of accents, and also a difference*

---

15. *The Idea of a Theatre* (Garden City, New York: Doubleday & Co., 1953), p. 101.

*in enunciations. Some break up the word: "In-spec-tor." Some
speak rapidly, others with a drawl. Their reaction is an immediate
one and they do not speak in character. Anyhow, the audience
cannot make out who says what. They are all crowded into the sofa,
nearly ten of them. . . . Everybody speaks at once. Their remarks
are in chorus. . . . In such an environment . . . such a collection
of idiots.*[16]

As music — sometimes as sheer sound — auditory stimuli can
actually generate and define action. As Appia saw, music as a time
art is a means of making action in time specific, of defining action in
space. As music is objective in time, it can make movement
objective in space. It can control gesture and movement in the same
way that it controls time.

This conception is utopian, but it is theoretically sound. It offers
the single hope, in my view, that the playwright may finally control
the form of the expression of his image.

Abstract sound is especially useful for defining or generating special
emotional responses. When Harold Hansen attended a Kubuki drama
in Japan, he wrote me immediately afterward: "When the men howl
and cry, they do it with all the stops out. At the best moments it
was quite moving; I and the women around us were weeping quietly
but profusely. The stories are all very melodramatic. Conflict is
treated as non-violent; they go into dance when they have a
physically violent scene. . . . The voices are highly trained, and some
of the female impersonators did much more dancing than
speaking. . . . I'm told that the language is just as direct — although
repeatedly stated (like opera) — but if done correctly it has an
accumulative effect that has real impact." For Hansen, emotion-
generating sound transcended the need for its translation into
language-meaning.

My purpose here is to show that sound, not necessarily as music,
can be structured as an artistic experience. I have done this in

------

16. Quoted in Cole and Chinoy, *Directing The Play*, p. 260.

production, and I am interested and encouraged that a special theatre for sound, called Audium, has been established in San Francisco in which sounds of the environment are orchestrated into experience compositions.

There a listener sits in a circular theatre surrounded by sixty-one loud speakers placed above, below, and all sides of him. The production takes place in the dark. Here natural sounds are most frequently presented — freight trains, a child's voice, an engine racing, running water, a boat docking, a running stream, as well as electronically generated sound. Its producers create both humor and pathos, diversion and insight.

If we are to bring more imaginative sound techniques to traditional drama, we must, while maintaining the objective of a predetermined response, proceed with uncommon subtlety.

    a. We might select that sound which expresses how the pertinent character feels or how the audience should feel about him. There have been experiments in which high frequency sounds, inaudible to the conscious ear, has been directed at the audience in an attempt to generate a condition of irritation that would be appropriate to the perception of a scene.

    b. We can select sound that oppresses, or, conversely, sound that elevates — sound that has the effect of manipulating the muscles. A scream invariably generates an involuntary muscular reaction.

    c. We can exploit the natural sounds of a scene such as the heartbeat or breathing of the Emperor Jones, the clanking of armor, the echo of footsteps, or the sound of one texture rubbing against another. This technique is exploited brilliantly in television commercials. Other devices are humming — perhaps by Linda in *The Death of A Salesman*; the song of Berniece Sadie Brown, "His Eye is on the Sparrow," in *A Member of the Wedding* as she holds Frankie on her lap; or the screaming of Jocasta as she flees from her new knowledge that Oedipus is her son.

    d. We can use those sounds that convey symbolically meanings we understand through accepted conventions. The sound of a watch ticking always implies the passage of time or a condition of impatience, tension, or impending consequence.

e. By injecting sounds out of context we can give special emphasis to what transpires before or after. The movie *No Exit* made artful use of the sound created by the sudden rise and flapping of a window-shade.

f. Often the complete absence of sound is an effective contrast. With silence, as with space, we suggest time. A long silence creates the experience of a lengthy passage of time — a principle important to the success of *Waiting for Godot.*

g. And, of course, we will use, when appropriate, fashionable conventions such as the single cello string, breaking glass, a score of mounting intensity such as Ravel's *Bolero,* and amplified heartbeats.

To help the audience feel as well as hear palpable sound in a production of *The Innocents,* one director placed giant speakers directly beneath the auditiorium. As Miss Giddons exorcised the evil spirit from Miles, the sound technician resonated low frequencies through the building so subtly that the audience was not consicious of the sound or its vibrations. But it was carried to a state of high emotional intensity. No one remarked afterwards about the special effect, but no one was unmoved by the performance.

A meaning-net. *W-2 Form.* Brigham Young University.

11
IDEAS IN PRODUCTION

There is so much beauty in our world, in its textures, colors, sounds, and forms, doubled in meaning by unexpected juxtapositions, that I deplore conventional theatrical production which ignores that fact. Today's theatre is, as it has always been, concerned exclusively with human relationships. And because to depict or allude to man as essentially animal is novel and profitable, or probably because some see him only as that, it represents him that way. Predictably, it expresses that view primarily through language.

But, as we have seen, language tends to circumscribe thought. The Taoist philosopher Chuang-Tze said: "Words exist only because of meaning. But where can I find a man who has forgotten words so that I may speak with him?"

Analyses of human relations described in language tell me little of what I most want to learn. I know of not one demonstrable and inevitably recurring fact about human relationships. Some love those who abuse them; some hate those who do not. Recently a counselor told a friend that she rejects her husband because she romantically loves her father. Even if true, which cannot be demonstrated, that statement has no practical value for her. Even believing it, she has not been able to improve her marriage.

It is time, then, in light of our new technology, to reconceive our art. Is theatre exclusively a medium for expressing through language today's dark view of man? Or is it also a new and unparalleled instrument for communicating "what is?" When we know what is, we shall know what may be, for what is is sublime, and what may be is perfection.

Close examination of any element reveals design, order, symmetry, synergism, a dependency of one part upon another for form. And the control of these qualities yields to man and therefore is good for his use. Color, sound, and sense-experience, when fragmented and structured, convey new experiences, wondrous sensations and useful meaning. Such — indeed all — elements are cemented by opposition or tension. Opposition is the mortar of the universe. Therefore, elements structured in tension are legitimate substance for theatre.

Today's theatre can — like Jackson Pollock's paintings, minimal art, or multimedia — weave nets of sense-stimuli in which the perceptor traps his own meaning. By close analysis through the technology of today it can depict, analyze, and celebrate the beauty and worth of our world.

Furthermore, when we preoccupy ourselves in production with conveying "what is," we ease the confusion about meaning. In the final analysis language can describe only the describable, and the purpose of art always was to transcend that objective. When theatre does rise to a poetic or metaphorical level, it has reached the place I envision here. The concrete theatre does not describe what was, or prescribe what might or should be; it conveys what is, what we can know today and here.

With this objective in view, and by means of the principles we have reviewed, we can project, in addition to traditional theatrical forms, productions having other aims and techniques.

We can conceive productions in which time is seen as a palpable cable. Aristotle spoke of a beginning, a middle, and an end — a structure paralleling the time continuum common to our experience. But if we bisect a time-cable, and, at our leisure, unsheath each of its strands one by one, we arrive at a new perception of ourselves and of our world. Our objective, then, may be to explore this moment — the now — to discover its sights, tastes, sounds, colors, and sensations. To perceive now is to live. To have no perception of now is to be dead.

This poem, "At Breakfast," written by May Swenson,[1] describes a common experience, one that most of us have each morning. But its beauty escapes us until she describes it.

Not quite
spherical
White
Oddly closed
and without a lid

---

1. Quoted with permission of the author from *To Mix with Time: New and Selected Poems* by May Swenson (New York: Charles Scribner's Sons, 1963).

A smooth miracle
here in my hand
Has it slid?
from my sleeve?

The shape
of this box
keels me oval
Heels feel
its bottom
Nape Knocks
its top

Seated
like a foetus
I look for
the dream-seam

What's inside?
A sun?

Off with its head
though it hasn't any
or is all head no body
a
One

Neatly
the knife scalps it
I scoop out
the braincap
soft
sweetly shuddering

Mooncream
this could be

Spoon
laps the larger
crescent
loosens a gilded
nucleus
from warm pap
A lyrical food

Opened
a seamless miracle
Ate a sun-germ
Good

Hers was a useful objective — to reveal forms and relationships that escape our common perception.

In structuring a comparable experience for theatre, we must avoid certain common errors:

1. We must not make the mistake of asking always what things mean. We will enjoy them for what they are. No one asks the meaning of a symphony. Some things are simply interesting. Some are beautiful in form. Red light on silver paper need not mean anything, but it is worth seeing; seeing it may increase our ability to see other beauty.

2. We must see that man is more than animal. He is architecture, form, mover, symbol, resonator, color, texture, possibly foe or friend, Eros, or beast. The human machine can be a thing of instructive beauty or a source of horror.

3. We must recognize that each sense's response can be orchestrated as we commonly do with sight (dance) and hearing (music). The technique consists of discovering the fundamental construct of a sense experience and then structuring that experience into theatrical form. A single taste, like a single sound, has implicit within it color, movement, and feeling. Even language, the most complex of sound, is structured from a single stimulus.

4. We must concede that man commonly views time chronologically but that some experiences can be developed

Movement-touch theatre.

cyclically or panoramically. I described in chapter four how to present four stories simultaneously.

Thus the substance of a concrete production might be to explore this moment. Its aim would be to discover its rhythm, movement, light, sight, sound, taste, language, feeling, so as to heighten awareness, perception, and appreciation for it.

To that end an audience with astute leadership might be taken through stretching, movement, or rhythm exercises — possibly even dances — designed to give it a new awareness of its physical self. These can be pleasurable and enlightening.

Or, some variation of the beautiful and satisfying Oriental custom of wrapping scented woods in elaborate and aesthetic packaging can be devised. Such packages are, in Japan, slowly unwrapped with great ceremony and visual appreciation at a social gathering, after which the wood is passed among the participants so that its texture, form, and scent can be appreciated.

After the audience has responded, more expert dancers or movers can move before it slowly or rapidly under changing temperatures and colors of light so as to catch and reveal the plastic beauty of human form.

I find it artful to insert "silent movies," using pantomime under stroboscopic lights, as an entertaining way of revealing human architecture under stop-action lighting. The plots are traditional and comic, but the visual effect is startling and informative. These units depict man as a depersonalized figure, without color, facial detail, or continuous motion, and in those circumstances generate a new appreciation for his form and action.

In addition, the serving of sharply flavored foods such as cinnamon, licorice, sour candy, even marshmallows, and pickles — especially if contrasted with sprayed scents of orange, lime, lemon and flowers — awakens the sense of taste.

Try leading the audience through the perception of progressively more complex sound. Amplify the sound of a single cello string, pick up its overtones in the sounds of the sea, move then to the sounds of turbulent weather, thence to language (a child's voice

174

reading a poem, possibly), thence to a richer language experience such as a quadraphonic sound-play presented in total darkness, and from thence to complex traditional and modern musical sounds, and thus bring the audience to understand what is inherent in each sound it hears.

A logical next step is to relate the sound to movement. If we invite the audience to create rhythms and to sing with the actors while we fill the stage with baton twirlers moving in complementary rhythms, we have a transition. Then roll a trampoline on stage and display the jumpers' movements in general stage light, then in shafts of intense color, and finally in white and colored strobe lights. We're ready, then, for more elaborate lighting experiences.

The practice of fragmenting light is common but invariably interesting. Properly done it can be exciting, even inspiring. The white light of a moment contains every conceivable color. In our cyclic structure we can examine each one on as many surfaces as inventiveness permits. Go far beyond those elements of light that characterize a common hard-rock light-show. The effect of strobe lights, of laser beams, of ozlid projectors, of projections on screens, objects, and moving figures, when well structured, is endlessly fascinating and informative.

In such a production, the stage serves as a mental mirror reflecting a series of symbols, images, and impressions evoking half-forgotten sorrows, joys, and fears. The major dramatic question is not, "Will the hero catch the villain?" but, "Does it mean?" and especially "What does it mean to me?" It asks of the viewer: "Is it interesting, is it beautiful, is it significant, does it tell you more about yourself and your world?" Such is the tension that gives cohesion to the production.

It is singularly important to prepare the audience for what it is to experience. It is dishonest, in my view, to advertise a theatrical evening, attract an audience that expects a play having a beginning, a middle, and an end (during which time a major dramatic question will be established and resolved) and then inflict upon it a free-form, seemingly unstructured series of events. But if the audience is

Movement — rhytnm — architecture

176

given the least help, through advertising, program notes, judicious comments, tradition, or atmosphere, it will accept this form of theatre for what it purports to be. We can persuade it that the theatre need not always tell stories, that it need not always use actors or language, that we intend to introduce it to new and wondrous concepts.

Mies van der Rohe has said that "God is in the details." Theatre is a useful place for depicting them — the symmetry and beauty of a microscopic cell that becomes for some a metaphor for the symmetry and beauty of God. In our uncertain age, the need for answers to the question "Why?" is unparalleled. But where shall we find the answer? "Why?" is difficult to answer in our confused world of service stations, riots, miniskirts, and similar minutiae. We find some answers, however, in the order, complexity, and form of music, the visual and tactile detail of aesthetic architecture, the resonance of color and rhythm, the variety and beauty of the human form in motion, or in sculpture, light, paper, and the infinite moods of men.

The details of a romantic kiss are endlessly fascinating. An evening can be devised solely from variations on the theme of a kiss. It can be tender, erotic, humorous, or all of these. A creative person will recall voice and movement variations based on the human kiss — its moods, qualities, frequency, length, objectives atmospheres — and if his imagination lags, he can borrow inspiration from romantic poems describing it. More inspiration comes from that moment when Robert Browning kisses away the fears of Elizabeth Barrett, that delicate kiss recorded in her diary by Anne Frank, and the portentous quality of Othello's kiss of Desdemona as he says: "Ah, balmy breath, that dost almost persuade/Justice to break her sword. One more, one more. . . ."

Suppose we follow the example of Miss Swenson's poem "At Breakfast" and use the stage as a magnifier of details that escape the casual observer. We can, as creative directors, construct a theatre poem that presents concrete images aimed at each of the senses.

And suppose that we contrast, in a theatrical manner, elements of

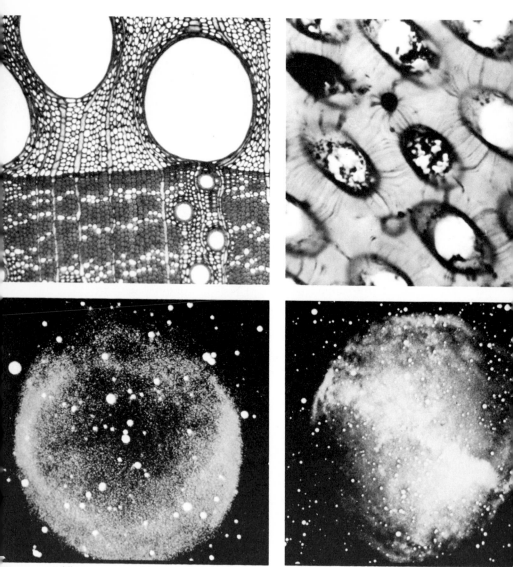

Micro-macro worlds converge. (NASA.)

179

the macro- and micro-world, leaving the spectator to derive what meaning he will. Let's choose from the phenomenal photographs of the solar system now available and project them on multiple screens including the floor or ceiling, and accompany the projections with appropriate music, thus establishing the magnitude of our theme. As a transition let's create a poem, given by a child in a tree, who examines himself and his world and marvels about the beauty and complexity of both:

> I may be
> awfully high
> here in my poplar tree.
> Still I wonder
> If there isn't someone
> higher up than I am
> in a taller poplar,
> looking down at me?
> — Dennis Smith

This transition will lead smoothly into an analysis of the complex rhythms found in our world, and it justifies a musician, dancer, or rhythm expert who will stand before the audience, lead it through rhythm experiences, and direct its attention to what he wants it to observe.

The audience will then be receptive, with an appropriate transition, to a review of the intricacies of movement. This may be a dance or a movement performance that proceeds smoothly from the audience rhythm unit that preceded it. This segment will have a beginning, a middle, a climax, and an end, and can be rich in appeal and meaning if the movement is added upon by the manipulation of the laws of optics. Change light, color, focus, intensity, and sounds — whether by projecting on screens, or, possibly, as with Alwin Nicolai, by projecting on the actors' bodies.

To maintain continuity, the action can return to the child who again questions the structure of matter, including the matter of nature — possibly the texture, color, and odor of the world's flowers.

Flowers provide a superlative opportunity to lead the audience from an analysis of detail to an appreciation for the general. One can begin with colorful and aesthetic photographs of their cellular structure which, when properly displayed, illustrates the awesome complexity of the floral micro-world. The audience at first will not know or understand what it is seeing, but it will enjoy the pure beauty of the forms it sees. In my view this extended study should be presented with as much sophistication as possible; the subject hints of the meaning of life. The audience would be surrounded by projections — required to observe three to seven or eight rapidly changing screens simultaneously. As we progress, projections become more general — eventually reaching a point where the audience sees not cells but petals, then full flowers, finally glorious panoramas of the exotic floral world.

If the development of the event is carefully and richly — which is to say complexly — constructed, the audience achieves a sense of having analyzed and reconstructed one of the world's universally loved objects. Of course, music will be carefully integrated so as to reinforce the constructive nature of the performance. In addition, social comment can be injected if one must be fashionable by introducing contrasting images of flowerless, colorless, polluted, pathetic views of the world, documenting the absence of these beautiful visions, and, possibly, charging us with responsibility for cultivating and preserving those now extant.

We can integrate entertaining silent movie sequences with the changing images on the screens. A story depicting young lovers who move from screen to screen plucking flowers from the projected images and transferring them from one to another and to other projected sequences would be romantic, charming, and timely.

Furthermore, the emphasis on light, which projections and the silent movies' flickering strobe create, can expand into an ambitious lighting experience. It is possible, I know, to hold an audience breathless while a human figure is freed from many layers of fabric,

Projected details construct architectural art. Brigham Young University Theatre piece. Lael J. Woodbury, director. Wallace M. Barrus, photographer.

if the textures of the fabric are interesting and the lights are changing, colorful, and intense. Or perhaps a conventional package wrapped in fabric or paper can justify moving textures and colors under light. One transcendent experience is merely to view silver lamé under intense blue, magenta, gold, green, white, crimson, purple, and orange. The experience is intensified, afterward, by manipulating the same fabric under contrasting colors directed simultaneously at opposite sides of it.

An audience enjoys participating physically. It will, if invited, dance, move, sing, and make sounds and rhythms. Or we can lead it through the photographic projection, the actual construction, or an explanation of the creation of an eight-foot glass or plexiglass construction or sculpture. This act will focus audience attention, if content of the finished sculpture expresses it, upon the theme of the production depicted there. The production's unity will be further stabilized by returning periodically to the child who ponders the great and the small of the earth.

We will move through as much of the micro-world as time and our inventiveness permit. We can explore each of our senses and structure our conclusions into dramatic form. Within the context of what I have described, I would present a photographic analysis of architecture, bringing, through color projections, those details of architecture that ordinarily escape our eye. We could define the delicate beauty of the curve of a banister, the texture of carpet, ornate carving on a doorknob or balustrade, a stained-glass window. The shadow of sun across granite or the odd form of configurations seen from unusual angles generates a new appreciation for architectural details that spectators usually ignore.

Our strategy is to show enough details to charm, interest, and quicken the audience but to structure those details so that our display of the complete, recognizable building appears at the same moment that the audience conceptualizes the details we have shown.

This joyous discovery, this sense of construction, this triumph of discovering that the details the audience has seen do indeed constitute aesthetic architectural form is the evening's climax. If we then move from full and glorious views of that entire building to views of it under changing seasons, periods, weather, light, and sun, night, and moon effects, it is simple, then, to move away from the building until we reveal the entire landscape, the horizon, the earth, the heavens, the solar system, and eventually the cosmic patterns with which our production began. Obviously, the musical or sound accompaniment to this entire sequence is as important as the visual and other sense-images presented.

Thus we generate knowledge and awe from details. By creating theatre art inversely, from meaning to conception, we can rekindle within the spectator a proper perception of the beauty of his world and a heightened sense of his own dignity and personal worth.

Die Soldaten. From Jarka Burion's *Scenography of Josef Svoboda.* Wesleyan University Press, 1

SUMMARY

Is theatre, then, essentially a playwright's language art that actors present in a performance area? Or does it remain a language art only because language was its chief agent for most of 2,500 years? Do the new media of today's technology merely refine and extend traditional theatre, or do they in fact invite a new form of art — one that expresses concepts as a mosaic orchestration of concrete sensory stimuli somewhat parallel to the composer's use of sound, the experimental film maker's light, and dancer's movement, the abstract painter's color, and the architect's space?

To answer these questions objectively, we must, as Kuleshov did with film, first determine the irreducible essence, the fundamental construct of theatre art — the most basic substance from which the artist, by whatever name, builds his work. From that perspective we see language, not as an essence, but as an adjunct of theatre that necessarily must be made concrete. That concrete expression of a concept is theatre art. The elements for making language concrete, sensory stimuli, are theatre's fundamental construct, and the creative director, because he is master of their significance and manipulation, may orchestrate them into sublime and innovative works.

By working inversely, by examining constructs closely for the meanings they contain, he can expand, repeat, focus, rearrange, distort, shade, and amplify them so as to monitor the audience's perception of them and bring it artfully to a reasonably predetermined response.

These new art mosaics, usually cyclic in form, perhaps will remain as episodes or movement until we develop the expertise with which to devise sustained and substantial works. A simple statement of structure might look like the chart on the following page.

Macro World Joy

	Subject	Time	Visual	Sound	Lights
1.	The Universe	1½	Planets	Nelson	Slides only
2.	Poem #1	45 sec	Dancer Luke	Nelson	Tree effect
3.	Audience Rhythms	2 min	Winterton	Winterton	General & projections
4.	Poem #2	60 sec	Smith	None	Tree
5.	Movement — optics	90 sec	Winterton	Electronic	Strobe
6.	Flower Show	3½	Slides only	Nelson	Projectors
7.	Song	2 min	Singer	Own	Color pool
8.	Silent Movie	2½	Company	Organ	Strobe
9.	Poem #3	90 sec	Luke	Smith	Tree
10.	Color and Texture	2½	Farmer	Farmer	Four beams
11.	Music Improvisations	3 min	Musicians	Nelson	General
12.	Audience Dance	8 min	Participants	Winterton	General
13.	Movements-optics	2 min	Winterton	Percussion	Projections
14.	Silent Movie	3 min	Company	Piano	Strobe
15.	Voice Collage	4 min	Actors	Smith	Color specials
16.	Poem #4	1 min	Luke	None	Tree
17.	Build Glass Sculpture	4 min	Sculpture	Nelson	Color pools
18.	Reveal Glass	90 sec	Glass	Nelson	Color specials
19.	Space Study	4 min	Slides	Electronic	Projectors
20.	Color Show	2 min	Fabrics	Farmer	Special
21.	Architecture	3½	Slides only	Farmer	Projectors
22.	Universe	3 min	Cells to planets	Nelson	12 projectors
23.	Finale	3 min	actors-mass chant	Luke	Color pools

A more sophisticated score for a mosaic theatre production may look something like the sketch on the following pages, prepared in full color by L. Moholy-Nagy.[1]

However we use them, our perpetual analyses of the artistic ramifications of each sensory stimulus will better qualify the theatre director to express conceptions artfully — whether his own or another's, whether in traditional or abstract forms.

---

1. Reproduced by permission.

MOHOLY-NAGY'S CHART

In Moholy-Nagy's sketch the stage is divided into three parts:

The lower part is for the larger forms and movements. This is Stage I. Stage II *(above Stage I), with a folding glass screen, is for smaller forms and more restricted movements. (The glass screen functions at the same time as a* screen for films *projected from the rear of the stage.) On III, the intermediate stage, are mechanical instruments, mostly without sounding boards or sound boxes, but with megaphones, for percussion, wind instruments, sound effects, noisemakers. Some of the stage walls are covered with a double layer of white canvas which transmits and diffuses colored lights from spots and beacons. The first and second columns of the score indicate, in vertical continuity, form and motion sequences. The third column shows successive light effects; the breadth of the strips signifies duration. Blackness = darkness. The narrow vertical stripes within the broad strip signify simultaneous illumination of parts of the stage. The fourth column is intended for music, which is only barely suggested here. The colored vertical stripes indicate various kinds of siren sounds which accompany a large part of the performance. Synchronism can be read horizontally from the score.*[2]

Sequence:

1st Column		2nd Column	3rd and 4th Columns
Arrows Plunge	Gigantic Apparatus	Arrows Plunge	Are Understandable
Louvered Shutters	Swing	Louvered Shutters	Without
Open Up	Flash	Open Up	Captions
Disks Rotate	Grids Widen	Disks Rotate	
Electric Apparatus	Wheels		
Lightning Thunder	Explosions	Film Projected On	
Grid Systems Of	Odors	Daylight Screen	
Colors	Clownery	Running Backward	
Shoot Up Down	Mechanized Men	Action	
Back Forth		Tempo	
Phosphorescence		Wild	

---

2. Walter Gropius, ed. *The Theatre of the Bauhaus* (Middletown, Connecticut: Wesleyan University Press, 1961), p. 48.

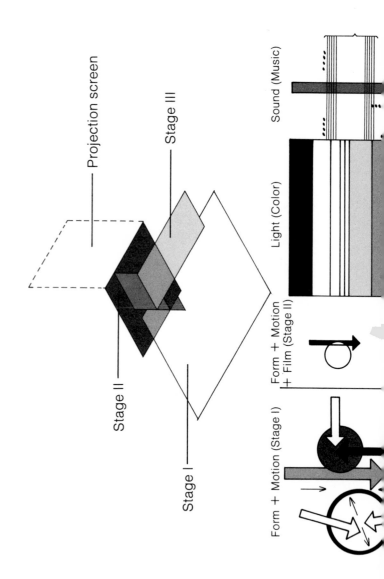

Projection screen

Stage III

Stage II

Stage I

Sound (Music)

Light (Color)

Form + Motion + Film (Stage II)

Form + Motion (Stage I)

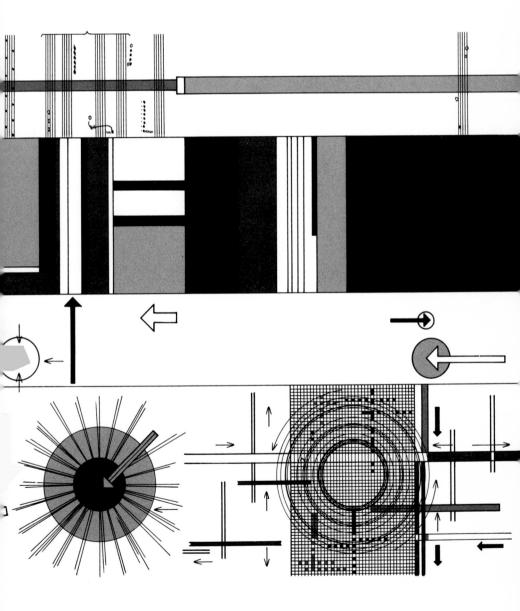

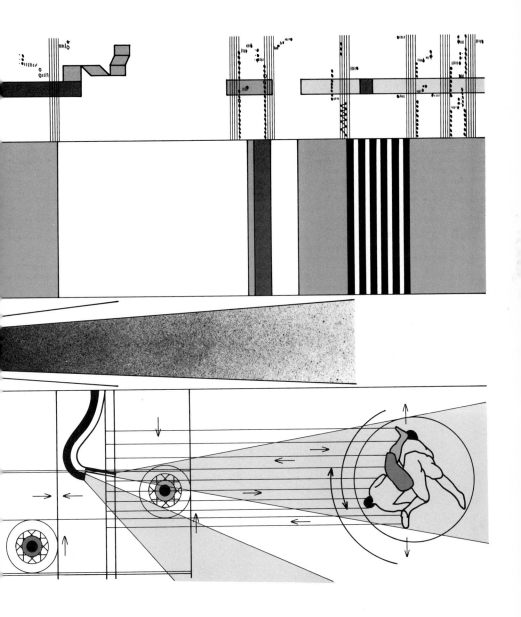

193

SELECTED AUTHORS AND WORKS CITED

Albee, Edward (1928–). "The Talk of the Town." *The New Yorker*. 19 December 1964. A playwright born in Washington, D.C., Albee attended Trinity College in Hartford, Connecticut, after graduating from Choate School. His literary honors include the Vernon Rice Memorial Award, 1960, for *The Zoo Story;* Best Plays of the 1960–61 season by the Foreign Press Association in New York for his plays *Death of Bessie Smith* and *The American Dream;* the Lola D'Annunzio Award, 1961, for his "sustained accomplishments in original playwrighting"; the New York Critics award for *Who's Afraid of Virginia Woolf?;* the American National Theatre and Academy Award; Foreign Press Association awards; five Tonys; and three Outer Circle Critics awards.

Appia, Adolphe (1862–1928). *The Work of Living Art.* Translated by H. D. Albright. And *Man is the Measure of All Things.* Translated by Barnard Hewitt. Coral Gables: University of Miami Press, 1960. The importance of Appia's theories of theatre as a "living art" is monumental. His concept of the human body as the theatre's essential energizing construct, controlled by music, revealed by light, and surrounded by an expressive — not imitative — milieu, revolutionized theatrical theory and liberated the thrust of the modern para-language theatre. *The Work of Living Art* is the most comprehensive statement of his theories. It deserves careful and repeated study. Born, reared, and educated in Geneva, Switzerland, he studied music in major European cities — especially at Bayreuth. He began publishing his theories as early as 1895, but except when collaborating with Eurythmic master Emile Jaques-Dalcroze, he presented few staged expressions of them. During his lifetime he was most active as an innovative master of theatrical design, but his influence as a theorist continues to expand in proportion to the publication of his translated writings.

Arnheim, Rudolph (1904–). *Art and Visual Perception.* Berkeley: University of California Press, 1954. An educator as well as a writer, Arnheim was born in Berlin, Germany. His study and training were done at the University of Berlin, where he received his Ph.D. in 1928. He was awarded a Guggenheim fellowship from 1942 to 1943. He served as professor at Sarah Lawrence College from 1943 to 1968.

This work discusses the virtues of vision and how to refresh and direct them. In it, Arnheim approaches the study of art through psychology. The experiments he cites and the principles of his thinking are derived largely from gestalt theory. The boo.., which should be read by every theatrical director, deals with what can be seen by everybody. Arnheim's theories and explanations are simple and straightforward and are illustrated with abundant examples.

Artaud, Antonin (1896–1948). *The Theatre and its Double.* Translated by Mary Caroline Richards. New York: Grove Press, 1958. Described by Jean-Louis Barrault as "the most important thing that has been written about the theatre in the twentieth century," this work is the fullest statement of Artaud's revolutionary, antilanguage theories. His passionate vision of a new and truly living theatre led him to eschew traditional social values and even language as devoid of truth and vitality. Instead he posited a theatre of emotional saturation based on symbol and ritual. French poet, actor, director, and playwright, as well as theorist, Artaud is, with Adolphe Appia, the supreme visionary of the modern theatre.

Bergson, Henri (1859–1941). "Laughter." *Comedy.* Garden City, New York: Doubleday and Co., 1956. Philosopher, born in Paris, Bergson opposed mechanism and determinism and vigorously asserted the importance of intuition. He represented France in diplomatic missions to Spain and the United States during World War I and was active in the League of Nations. In 1927 he received the Nobel prize in literature. His works include: *Time and Free Will,* 1889; *Matter and Memory,* 1896; *Introduction to Metaphysics,* 1903; *Creative Evolution,* 1907; and *The Two Sources of Morality and Religion,* 1932.

Canfield, Curtis (1903–). *The Craft of Play Directing.* New York: Holt, Rinehart, and Winston, 1963. This book describes the craftsmanship of the director, especially the director's functions, qualifications, and areas of responsibility. Some tested methods of play analysis and staging are illustrated, and ways are suggested for approaching individual and ensemble problems in acting. A step-by-step progression is followed from the director's first reading of the manuscript through the different stages of preparation and to the final performance. A useful, traditional, directing text.

Clark, Barrett (1890–1953). *European Theories of the Drama,* rev. ed. New York: Crown Publisher, 1947. Author and editor, Clark was an organizer of the Dramatists' Play Service, which leases plays to nonprofessional theatres. From 1936 until his death he served as the Play Service's executive director. Born in Toronto, he taught for some years at Columbia University.

Clay, James H. (1927–), and Krempel, Daniel (1926–). *The Theatrical Image.* New York: McGraw-Hill Book Co., 1967. Professors Clay, of Brandeis University, and Krempel, of Syracuse University, describe here, with authority and persuasion, that essential process in theatrical art that takes place *before* rehearsals begin. They presume that it is a director's art to make a playwright's vision concrete on the stage, and they theorize about how to derive that vision from the written play.

Cole, Toby (1916–), and Chinoy, Helen Krich (1922–). *Directing the Play.*
Indianapolis: The Bobbs-Merrill Co., 1953. This book is a superb anthology of
famous directors' theories, including a lengthy essay on the history of the art of
directing by Chinoy. One section contains fifteen statements by directors such
as André Antoine, Vsevolod Meyerhold, and Tyrone Guthrie about their artistic
values and craft. The final section of the book contains rehearsal logs, directors'
workbooks, and eyewitness reports of the work of such artists as Max Reinhardt,
Bertolt Brecht, and Elia Kazan. Prescribed reading.

Dean, Alexander (1893–1939). *Fundamentals of Play Directing.* New York: Holt,
1941. Dean, born in Newburyport, Massachusetts, was educated at Dartmouth
College and Yale University. He was a professional actor from 1917 to 1920,
an associate professor of dramatic art and literature in the School of Speech at
Northwestern University from 1923 to 1927, and an assistant director of Yale
University's University Theatre from 1929 to 1933. From 1934 until his death,
Dean served as managing director for the South Shore Players, Cohasset,
Massachusetts. His text is the standard work on the mechanical aspects of
directing.

This work, in its 1965 publication, was edited and expanded by Lawrence
Carra (1909–), who was born in Salina, Italy, and received his B.A. from Harvard
and his MFA from Yale in 1937. He has directed and produced for both theatre
and television. Carra served as a guest lecturer and director at Stanford (1945),
Indiana University (1951), Columbia (1956), and as a professor at Carnegie-
Mellon University.

Eisenstein, Sergei Mikhailovich (1898–1948). *Film Form.* New York: Harcourt,
Brace and Co., 1949. Soviet film director and theoretician, who achieved fame
for his political epics of the Russian revolution, Eisenstein was born in Riga and
studied architecture and engineering at St. Petersburg. During Russia's civil
war he acted in plays for the Bolshevik army, and afterwards he managed a
carnival and a small workers' theatre in Moscow. He was then appointed as
assistant director and chief dramatist for Proletcult Theatre, where he created
dramatizations and an experimental play, *Anti Jesus.* His first motion picture
was *Strike,* 1924, after which *Potemkin,* 1925; *Ten Days that Shook the World,*
1927; and *The General Line,* 1929. He worked abroad for several years,
including the United States, but returned to the Soviet Union in 1932. In 1940
he wrote this splendid study of film esthetics, *Film Form.* Thereafter he taught
classes in cinema technique at the Soviet Cinema Institute and worked with his
last great film, *Ivan the Terrible,* and his second theoretical work, *Film Sense.*

Fergusson, Francis (1904–). *Idea of a Theatre.* New York : Doubleday & Co., 1953.
Fergusson was born in Albuquerque, New Mexico. A professor of Comparative

Literature at Rutgers University, Fergusson published *Dante's Drama of the Mind* in 1952 and *The Human Image in Dramatic Literature* in 1957. He served as dramatic critic for *The Bookman* (1930–32) and taught at the New School for Social Research (1932–34), at Bennington College (1934–47), and at Indiana University (1952–53). He was a member of the Institute of Advanced Studies (1947–49), and he directed seminars in literary criticism at Princeton from 1949 to 1952.

Gibson, William (1914–). *The Seesaw Log.* New York: Alfred A. Knopf, 1959. Author and playwright, Gibson was born in New York City. He is presently president and cofounder of the Berkshire Theatre Festival in Stockbridge, Massachusetts. He received the Harriet Monroe Memorial Prize for a group of his poems published in *Poetry,* 1945; the Topeka Civic Theatre award for *A Cry of Players,* 1947; and the Sylvania award for his television play, *The Miracle Worker,* 1957. *The Seesaw Log* is a chronicle of the stage production in 1958 of his play, *Two for the Seesaw.* It is a moving and informative account of the creation of the playscript and the process and difficulties of presenting it on stage. He describes especially well the essential conflict between the language-nature of literature and the concrete stimuli-nature of theatre.

Gorelik, Mordecai (1899–). *New Theatres for Old.* New York: Samuel French, 1952. Designer, director and educator, Gorelik was born in Russia. He studied at the Pratt Institute in 1920. He was an instructor-designer at the School of Theatre, New York, and at the American Academy of Dramatic Arts. Since 1924, he has designed over forty professional productions, and he has served as a research professor in theatre at Southern Illinois University. This book, described as "one of the fifteen basic books" by *Theatre Arts Magazine,* shows vividly how new audiences with new values and perceptions demand new modes of art. It is essential reading for any theatrical director. The three articles by Gorelik cited in this work, published in *Player's Magazine* as a series, describe Gorelik's techniques for determining the meanings of a play, or the vision that generated it. This series should be read in conjunction with Clay and Krempel's *The Theatrical Image* cited above.

Gropius, Walter (Adolf) (1883–1969), ed. *The Theatre of the Bauhaus.* Middletown, Connecticut: Wesleyan University Press, 1961. A German architect who was born in Berlin, Gropius taught that form should follow function in architecture, industrial design, and city planning. He founded the Bauhaus School of Design in 1919 which the Nazis closed in 1933. He served as chairman of the Department of Architecture at Harvard from 1938 to 1952 and was thereafter active in his firm, the Architects' Collaborative. Some of his other literary works include: *Rebuilding Our Communities,* 1946; *The New Architecture and the*

Bauhaus (trans. by T. M. Shand), 1935; and *Internationale Architektur,* 1925. Lazlo Moholy-Nagy (1895–1946), who contributed "Theatre, Circus, Variety" to this work, and who also wrote *Vision and Motion,* was a painter, author, photographer, and cinema director. He was born in Hungary. He graduated in law from the University of Budapest in 1915. In 1937 Moholy-Nagy came to the United States, and from 1939 to his death, he was president of the Institute of Design in Chicago. He is known for his experimental work with light and color in painting, photography, and film.

Oskar Schlemmer (1888–1943) contributed "Man And Art Figure" to *The Theatre of Bauhaus.* He is one of the distinguished German artists of the twentieth century. He believed that art should bring about a new way of seeing the world both in form and idea. His essay in *The Theatre of the Bauhaus* describes theoretical and production analyses of the architectural form of the human body.

Grube, Max (1854–1934). *Geschichte der Meinger.* Stuttgart: Deutsche Verlags-Anstalt, 1926. Born in Dorpat, Germany, Grube attended school in Berlin and obtained his first position as a professional actor with the Meininger Court Theatre. During his career as an actor and director, Grube wrote poems, plays, and books on theatre history.

Guthrie, Tyrone (1900–1971). "Shakespearean Production." *The Year's Work in the Theatre: 1949–1950.* London: Longsmans, Green, 1950. Born in Tunbridge Wells, England, Guthrie earned a B.A. at Oxford. He was chancellor of Queen's University at Belfast from 1936 until his death. He was knighted in the New Year Honors in 1961. Eminent for his directing of Shakespearean and ancient Greek dramas, Sir Guthrie also founded the Tyrone Guthrie Theatre, Minneapolis, Minnesota.

Hewitt, Barnard (1906–). *Theatre U.S.A.* New York: McGraw-Hill Co., 1959. This distinguished theatre historian surveys here the professional theatre in the United States from its beginning to the present. He tells its story primarily through contemporary accounts and interprets that story by commentary that places and amplifies the eyewitness accounts and describes patterns of change in American drama, acting, scenery, lighting, costuming, theatre building, and audience. Many of the book's selections are reviews of performances. They include descriptions of important events such as the Astor Palace riot and the Iroquois Theatre fire. The book is useful to all students of the American theatre and is interesting also to the general reader.

Hollingworth, Harry Levi (1880–1956). *Psychology of the Audience.* New York: American Book Co., 1935. Born in DeWitt, Nebraska, Hollingworth obtained his

B.A. from the University of Nebraska and his doctorate from Columbia. He was the author of many books and papers in journals of psychology, education, and social science. In 1907, he joined Columbia University, and at his retirement in 1946 he was head of the Department of Psychology at Barnard.

Houghton, Charles Norris (1909–), ed. *Laurel Masterpieces of Continental Drama.* New York: Dell Publishing Co., 1963. Born in Indianapolis, Houghton received his A.B. from Princeton and his DFA from Dennison University. Presently Dean of Theatre Arts for the State University of New York at Purchase, Houghton has published *Moscow Rehearsals,* 1936; *Advance From Broadway,* 1941; *But Not Forgotten,* 1951; *Return Engagement,* 1962.

Humphrey, Doris (1895–1958). *The Art of Making Dances.* New York: Holt, Rinehart, and Winston, 1959. American dancer and choreographer, born in Oak Park, Illinois, Humphrey's work is characterized by her faith in the power of dance to ennoble the life of man. Her contribution to the development of expressive dance is profound. When in 1945 she retired as a dancer, she became artistic director of the Jose Limon Company. In 1955 she founded the Julliard Dance Theatre, for which she restaged works from her repertory and created new ones. After many years of teaching dance technique, she taught annual courses in the art of choreography. Her theories of dramatic structure and space utilization are useful to the theatre director.

Hunt, Hugh (1911–). *The Director in the Theatre.* New York: Holt, Rinehart, and Winston, 1959. Born in England, Hunt obtained his B.A. and M.A. at Oxford. From 1969 to 1971 he was director of The Abbey Theatre, Dublin. He has authored plays and books on the theatre, and he now serves as professor of drama at the University of Manchester, England.

Huxley, Aldous Leonard (1894–1963). *History of Tension. Annals of the New York Academy of Sciences.* Edited by Otto V. St. Whitelock, vol. 67, May 1957. New York: The Academy, 1957. Huxley was an English novelist and essayist. He once intended to become a physician, but failing eyesight persuaded him to study English Literature and philology at Oxford, where he graduated in 1915. Eventually he moved to America, residing in Southern California, where he continued his writing career. His works include: *Antic Hay,* 1923; *Brave New World,* 1932; *The Perennial Philosophy,* 1945; and *The Devils of London,* 1952. This provocative essay on tension is useful in understanding dramatic structure.

Jaques-Dalcroze, Emile (1865–1950). *Rhythm, Music and Education.* Translated by Harold F. Rubenstein. New York: G.P., Putnam's Sons, 1921. Born in Vienna, Jaques-Dalcroze studied composition and eventually became a professor of harmony at the Geneva Conservatory in 1892. He was founder of schools of eurhythmics in London, Paris, Venice, Stockholm, and New York. Eurhythmics is a term used to designate the representation of musical rhythms by bodily movements. The idea underlying Dalcroze's music education system is to teach children to know themselves, to measure their intellectual and physical capabilities, and to submit them to exercise enabling them to use their powers. *Rhythm, Music, and Education* is the story of the author's research, failures, and definite achievements in his theory of Eurhythmics. In chronological order the chapters of his book record his ideas as expressed in lectures and articles.

Kandinsky, Wassily (1866–1974). *Concerning the Spiritual in Art.* New York: George Wittenborn, 1912. This Russian painter and graphic artist was one of the masters of modern art and was the outstanding representative of purely abstract painting that dominated the first half of the twentieth century. He began his studies at the University of Moscow in law and economics but in 1896 started his artistic work. He attended the Azbe School of Painting in Munich, and after returning to Russia, he taught at the University of Moscow, then became Vice-President of the Academy of Arts, which he founded in 1921. Changing Soviet attitudes toward art motivated him to leave Russia that year. Eventually he took out German, then French, citizenship while continuing his teaching and painting.

Kepes, Gyorgy (1906–). *Language of Vision.* Chicago: Paul Theobald and Co., 1959. An author, painter, and educator, Kepes was born in Selyp, Hungary. He received an MFA in Budapest. In Berlin Kepes worked closely with Moholy-Nagy, the Hungarian painter, designer, and photographer, on films, stage sets, and graphic designs. In 1946, Kepes became professor of visual design in the School of Architecture and Planning at the Massachusetts Institute of Technology. In 1967 he was made director of the Center of Advanced Visual Studies. This provocative study of how we see should be reviewed by all creators of space arts.

Langer, Susanne K.(1895–). *Philosophy in a New Key.* New York: New American Library, 1948. *Feeling and Form.* New York: Charles Scribner's Sons, 1953. Born in New York City, Langer received both her M.A. and her Ph.D. from Radcliffe. The mathematician and philosopher Alfred North Whitehead, her friend and tutor, led her into the study of symbolic logic. Since 1945 she has taught at Columbia University. *Philosophy in a New Key* postulates that philosophy is a new key, and she tries to show how the main themes of our thought tend to be transposed into it. The reorientation of philosophy taking place in our age provides a new perspective on the ideas and arguments of the past. *Feeling and Form,* as a sequel to the above, describes her critique of art and science based on an analysis of discursive symbolism.

Lanz, Henry (1886–1945). *The Physical Basis of Rime.* London: Oxford University Press, 1931. Born in Moscow, Lanz attended the Imperial University of Moscow and obtained his Ph.D. from Heidelberg in 1912. Concentrating on philosophy, Lanz became a professor of Slavic languages and philosophy at Stanford University. He has written in the areas of Slavic literature, ethics, and epistemology. This book is the result of the author's studies in logic. He extends the strategic positions of modern realism beyond pure logic and applies its principles to esthetics. In that exercise, he accumulates new experimental and bibliographical material dealing with rhythm and rime, and attempts to organize his views to the consistency of a theory.

Littlewood, Joan (1914–). "Theatre or Fun Palace?" *Playbill,* vol. 2, no. 4. April 1965. Born in London, Littlewood has directed some 150 stage productions, many of which were produced at the Theatre Workshop, Theatre Royal, Stratford, London. She has received high honors for acting, production, and direction.

Mamoulian, Rouben (1897–). "Rhythm, Music, and Theatre," *Etude,* 63. April 1945. A director, writer, and producer, Mamoulian was born in Georgia, Russia. He has directed and produced many operas, operettas, and musical presentations. He has written and published the book *Abigayl,* 1964, and has received many awards, including the first prize in 1931 at the Venice International Film Festival for *Queen Christina,* and the New York Film Critics award in 1936 for best direction of the year for *The Gay Desperado.*

Marowitz, Charles (1934–). "Learlog," *Tulane Drama Review,* 8. Winter, 1963. Director and author, born in New York City, Marowitz's first production was *Doctor Faustus* in 1948 at the Labor Temple Theatre, New York City. He collaborated with Peter Brook in the experimental "Theatre of Cruelty" season, 1964. He has since directed *The Trigon,* 1964; *Hamlet, The Bellow Plays, Loot,* 1966; *Fanghorn,* 1967; *Fortune and Men's Eyes,* 1968; *MacBeth, Blue Comedy, Muzeeka and the Fan War,* 1969; *Chicago|Conspiracy, Palach,* 1970; and *The Critic as the Artist,* 1971. Since 1955 he has been a critic for *The Village Voice.*

Meyer, Leonard B. (1918–). *Emotion and Meaning in Music.* Chicago: The University Press, 1956. Born in New York, Meyer obtained his B.A. and M.A. from Columbia University, then his Ph.D. from the University of Chicago in 1954. Since 1961 he has served as a professor of music at the University of Chicago. This examination of the problem of musical meaning and its communication yields useful insights into the general problems of meaning and communication, especially those having aesthetic dimensions.

Miller, Arthur (1915–). "Arthur Miller Ad-Libs on Eliz Kazan," *Show*. January 1964. Born in New York City, Miller graduated in 1938 with an A.B. from the University of Michigan. He worked with the short-lived Federal Theatre Project, then wrote radio scripts for several network programs. His honors include the Theatre Guild National Playwrighting Contest, 1st award, 1938; the Hopwood Award, University of Michigan, 1936, 1937; the New York Drama Critics Circle award, 1947, for *All My Sons;* the Pulitzer Prize in Drama, 1949, and a second Circles award for *Death of a Salesman;* and the Antoinette Perry Award, 1953. His literary works include: *All My Sons,* 1947; *Death of a Salesman,* 1949; *The Crucible,* 1953; *View from the Bridge,* 1955; *The Misfits,* 1961; *After the Fall,* 1965; and *I Don't Need You Anymore,* 1967.

O'Neill, Eugene (1888–1953). "On Stage He Played the Novelist," *The New York Times Book Review*. 30 August 1964. Educated at Princeton and Harvard, O'Neill was awarded the Nobel Prize for Literature in 1936. He is thought by many to be America's foremost dramatist.

Prince, Harold (1928–). *Contradictions*. New York: Dodd, Mead and Co., 1974. Born in New York City, Prince obtained a B.A. at the University of Pennsylvania. Beginning as an assistant stage manager for *Tickets Please,* he produced, in partnership with F. Brisson and R. E. Griffith, *The Pajama Game,* 1954; *Damn Yankees,* 1955; and *New Girl in Town,* 1957. With Griffith he produced *West Side Story,* 1957, *Fiorello,* 1959; *Tenderloin,* 1960; and *A Call on Cuprin,* 1961. *Fiorello* received a Pulitzer Prize and the New York Drama Critics Circle award. Since then, his more well-known productions have been: *Take Her, She's Mine,* 1963; *A Funny Thing Happened on the Way to the Forum,* 1963; *Fiddler on the Roof,* 1964; *Follies,* 1971; and *A Little Night Music,* 1973.

Seashore, Carl (1866–1949). *Psychology of Music*. New York: McGraw-Hill, 1938. Born in Sweden, Seashore received his Ph.D. from Yale in 1895. He received a Mus.D. from the Chicago Music College in 1939. From 1908 to 1937, he was head of the psychology department at the State University of Iowa. This book advocates a scientific approach to the study of music.

Southern, Richard (1912–). *The Open Stage*. London: Faber and Faber, 1943. Born in England, Southern was educated at Bailliol College, Oxford, and has been President of St. John's College, Oxford, since 1969. In *The Seven Ages of the Theatre,* 1961, he discusses theatre history in terms of the actual structures and geographic places where theatre has been enacted.

Stanislavski, Constantin (1863–1938). *Building A Character*. Translated by
Elizabeth Reynolds Hapgood. New York: Theatre Arts Books, 1949. Born in
Moscow, Stanislavski studied from 1878 to 1881 at the Lazarez Institute of
Oriental Languages. In 1888, he helped found the Society of Art and Literature,
whose aim was to bring together workers from all spheres of art for the
systematic presentation of good plays. In 1898, Stanislavski, with Vladimir
Nemirovich-Danchenko, founded the Moscow Art Theatre. Here, he tried to do
away with stereotyped mannerisms. The Moscow Art Theatre became the home
of theatrical naturalism. Unlike his *An Actor Prepares,* this book describes some
of his views about the technical aspects of the actor's art. It is an inspiring,
informative work.

Thorndike, Sybil (1882–). "Sybil Thorndike Talking to Derek Prouse," *The Sunday
Times Magazine Section (London).* 8 July 1962. Born in England, Thorndike
attended the Guildhall School of Music in London and studied for the stage at
Ben Greet's Academy in 1904. A prominent stage actress, Thorndike is known
for her leading roles in Shakespearean and classical repertoire. She is coauthor
with her brother of the biography, *Lilian Bayliss,* 1938.

Wagner, Richard (1813–83), in *European Theories of the Drama.* Edited by Barrett
Clark. Rev. ed. New York: Crown Publishers, 1947. Born into an artistic and
theatrical family, Wagner was a musical dramatist. After leaving Leipzig
University in 1833, he spent three years in Paris. In 1842 he obtained a
position at the court theatre of Dresden. After being exiled from Germany in
1849 because of his involvement in the 1848 revolution, Wagner wrote a series
of prose works outlining his theories of the aesthetic function of musical drama.
His great tetralogy, *Der Ring des Nibelungen (The Ring of the Nibelung),* 1876,
as well as some of his other works such as *Tristan und Isolde* and *Parisfal* are
examples of his attempts to create a new synthesized art form.

Webster, Margaret (1905–72). "Shakespeare and the Modern Theatre," the fifth
lecture of the Helen Kenyon Lectureship at Vassar College, delivered 1 June
1944. Webster descended from a 19th century theatrical family; she was the
daughter of Ben Webster and Dame May Whitty. A Shakespearean director, she
was especially acclaimed for her productions of *Richard II, Hamlet,* and
Twelfth Night.

INDEX